Male Perspectives on

THE VALUE
OF WOMEN
AT WORK

Also by Susan Popoola

Touching the Heart of Milton Keynes: A Social Perspective

Consequences: Diverse to Mosaic Britain

Male Perspectives on

THE VALUE OF WOMEN AT WORK

By SUSAN POPOOLA

Male Perspectives on The Value of Women at Work
© Susan Popoola 2021
ISBN: 978-1-8380989-1-9
Cover Design: Ope Aluko

First published in 2021 by Mosaic Gold Ltd
Wood View House
Medbourne Park, Milton Keynes, UK
MK5 6FF
contact@MosacGold.org
www.MosacGold.org

Printed by Ingram Spark UK and USA

Dedicated to the amazing men that have contributed to this book, together with all the amazing men in my own life.

In the fight for women's rights,
the support of men remains crucial.

Hilary Clinton.

#Selah

Contents

MALE PERSPECTIVES ON

THE VALUE OF WOMEN AT WORK

Prologue

My most fundamental belief is we all as human beings have value and something to contribute to the world we live in, inclusive of the world of work. Unfortunately, there are marked disparities in how we are valued on the basis of gender and various other characteristics and features. There are a number of women's organisations, programmes, mentorship initiatives etc which are focused on supporting women. I recognise there are times when these interventions need to be exclusively for women. However, if we want men to fully understand the challenges women face so they are able to more effectively provide input and support, we need to find ways of including them in the dialogue more.

The Value of Women at Work is a way of including men by sharing the perspectives from men who try to support or advocate for women for the benefit of men that don't truly value women, understand or know how to. It's also for women to be presented with a positive view of themselves from men with some insights into to some of things that may get in their way: both external factors and things they could do differently.

I'm privileged to have had the opportunity to converse with a variety of different men on the subject of the Value of Women at

Work. I say I'm privileged because the men I spoke to ranging from the ages of 16 to a man in his early 70s come from a rich diversities of backgrounds and locations across different continents – providing a diversity of viewpoints. Most significantly, I see myself as privileged as they were all tremendously open and honest in their conversations with me.

I must emphasise as they did, that their comments are based on their personal perceptions and observations. They are generalisations which in no way represent all women. Sometimes I balked at things they had to say, but when I took time to reflect, I better understand where they were coming from. I don't agree with everything said, but I know they are all good, well intended men with a variety of levels of understanding and different perspective of women and their value in the world of work. I've therefore learnt from each of them and to each of them I am extremely grateful.

I am truly excited to share what they had to say with you as I believe it will be of great value to you too.

I believe men reading will better understand the female experience and how to better engage, support and enable us, thus bringing about changes that lead to a better work environment for everyone.

For women, I believe you will be encouraged in the knowledge that there are men that already see and support us and want to be our allies. You will also better understand both their perceptions of the world and as such how to more effectively navigate the work environment with the benefit of this knowledge.

I recommend reading what they have to say with an open mind. If you disagree with what they have to say or believe they simply don't understand, it would be easy to walk away. I'd like to suggest a different response. Understanding their thinking not only provides you with an understanding of some of the challenges and a better understanding

of how to navigate the work world as is; it also reinforces the need for greater dialogue with men that care so that they can better understand, advocate, provide their support and help bring about necessary change.
#Selah

Reflecting on The System

D r Tariq Siddique is a former General Practitioner. He has worked as a doctor in both the UK and Australia for over 25 years. His work has steered the development of cross-organisational working in Urgent Care. He has worked as a member of the Professional Executive Committee of countywide commissioning organisations providing leadership and vision for better care across Health and Social Care. He now works as a Leadership Coach with a strong interest in Gender and Race equality, additionally championing the cause of supporting the next generation of leaders.

Men's Presence & Ears

Tariq has always wanted to be involved in supporting women leaders in organisations that are often male dominated. In medicine, as in other areas of the workforce, there is a 50:50 split in the workforce by gender. However when you get to the echelon of leadership it is typically male dominated. Tariq remembers a conference he attended alongside around 600-700 medical professionals. A specific breakout session led by a friend that interested him was about Women Leaders in male dominated organisations. He was surprised that of the 80-90 participants that attended this particular breakout session he was the only male.

Tariq ponders on how women are going to be able to communicate and express their requirements and needs in the workplace if men are not actually listening to what's going on. In this case, there was a room of intelligent and experienced women. However, without the presence of men to understand what changes women require, it becomes an echo chamber. Tariq attended the session as he believes that there is a need for more male ears in the room during such conversations – emphasising ears as opposed to voices. One of Tariq's driving forces is to find where inequality sits within organisations; to question how it came about and help determine what can be done about it. This relates to areas such as ethnic minorities and LGBTQ issues as well as gender.

Tariq further believes there is a need for men to have a greater interest and awareness of the challenges. It's possible the impression was given that the session was for women. It may, however, have been a blind spot for a lot of men if they thought the conversation was not relevant to them. Tariq believes the conversations were very interesting and found the the women to be passionate about issues, but it was an echo chamber as everyone was agreeing with the issues raised with no one saying they were unaware of the issues raised, because the people (i.e. men that were unaware of the issues) were not in the room. This conference was for people in the medical profession. Tariq does not, however, believe what he observed is likely to be unique to the medical field.

Perceived Threats

Tariq also ponders on the perceived threats men may see to the male dominated hierarchies that have been created over time. When you break it down, it can become quite scary for some men. For instance, if we have equal gender representation right across the board, that means that a lot fewer men are required in those top positions, as some of those positions would be held by women to reflect the actual population. The women Tariq speaks of in his work are absolutely capable of being leaders in their organisations, yet there are blockages to them. He's unsure where the blockage comes from and ponders if it's an unconscious male bias with men not seeing the problem, because they don't see it as their problem. There's also the further challenge of what would happen to several male executives if such changes were put in place.

Women's Value

Tariq believes that female leaders who have managed to get to the top levels within the NHS, at times display very male characteristics and can be quite aggressive, not listening and being rather dictatorial. It's not that his experience of women leaders is slighter lower in the organisations though. The female leaders that Tariq has come across, that he is more attuned to, are very collaborative. They listen. They look at the benefits for the whole organisation and are usually more focused on long term solutions rather than short-term fixes. They tend to collaborate outside of their organisations more and not just within their organisations. They tend to look at factors beyond what would be considered their normal remit. For instance, talking to adjacent organisations that might be experiencing similar issues; exploring how they can work together to find solutions. They also tend not to rush the decision making process as much as their male counterparts. They also network in a manner that comes across as very authentic, speaking to people because they are interested in them and not to determine what they can get from the person. This is not forgetting that not all men are the same, and Tariq has come across men who are exceptionally good at doing this as well. He does, however, find it to be more common with women.

Tariq brings some useful insight into the value that women bring to justify parity between men and women. He points out that if everybody within the organisational structure is of the same mould, problems will always be looked at in the same way with a focus on the same type of solution, missing out on alternate solutions which might be far more effective. Tariq believes we miss out on this with gender disparity at the decision making level due to the limited number of women at this level.

Barriers

Expanding on what prevents females from being represented at the senior level, Tariq speaks of what happens at both the conscious and subconscious levels. He believes that at the conscious level there is a judgement of value from male colleagues at the very senior level which is represented in the concern that women are not going to be committed as they are going to go off and have children and then come back to work on a part time basis. The belief is that as a result, women are unlikely to have as much experience as men and organisations are therefore probably better off choosing men. Tariq believes this is a dogmatic one-sided view of the issues, however, it is quite prevalent at senior levels of leadership where things are often viewed literally. What it doesn't account for, explains Tariq, is the lived experiences derived from being a parent or a mother. Instead, the focus is on the men who haven't taken time off: a short term view which doesn't value the contributions or experience gained from parenting. If you manage children, you can manage any boardroom. There are different characters and behaviours that are displayed in a boardroom. Viewed from the perspective of the Parent, Adult & Child Model of Transactional Analysis, you may see all displayed in a boardroom context. Sometimes behaviours can lead the boards to be quite dysfunctional. If you've had the experience of managing a number of children, either just yours or even just your child and friends, all displaying different behaviours and requiring attention at the same time, it takes a huge skillset to navigate through this. As a parent, most especially as a mother, you learn to do this. The same skillset is equally valid to manage a Board or in a wider leadership context. It's possible that senior male leaders who've worked quite intensively and in senior positions have not taken time off to take on the main child care responsibilities in their households. As a result, they don't have the same level of experience/skills in this area as women.

At the subconscious level, there is a strong view of what leadership should look like, which works on the assumption that certain characteristics are not suitable for leadership. Having reviewed leadership over 300-400 years and observed how it's changed over time, Tariq can observe that several communities were historically matriarchal societies in which the senior leaders were female. They were the mothers of the tribe. They had quieter characteristics and could negotiate with the tribe as a whole and neighbouring tribes, bringing about peaceful resolutions which minimised the risks to the tribe. When we go on to male leaders, most especially in the US and the

West, the leader is more often the person who speaks the fastest and loudest with the ability to get the last word in, at times at any cost. It's no longer the quiet leader who is the more thoughtful, but the one who is very much at the forefront. This change was very much reflected from the Industrial Revolution, with the male dominant figure taking the lead.

When viewed through this lens, another unconscious bias comes into play. The conclusion will be made that women don't typically have the skill sets common to a male model and so they don't get into senior positions except where women display similar skillsets to men. This, however, means that an alternative viewpoint on issues and solving problems is not then provided.

In the pre-industrial era the roles of men and women were actually more complimentary with the recognition that one without the other was unsuccessful as you needed the balance of the two. This is totally absent at senior organisation level. This is a threat to those organisations' long term sustainability and everything that runs in parallel to them. This runs across the board in health services, the private sector, political organisations and almost everywhere else within Western Society, particularly those places that are most male dominated. As a result, women often tend to reach a certain level and then have to change their behaviour to go further, unless they are absolutely exceptional and able to find their own unique approach. Within the British NHS, each hospital trust is a separate entity with its own Chief Executive and Board. The vast majority of these Executives are run by men. There are more female leaders in Community Trusts which do not seem to attract many men.

While recognising that his knowledge may be limited as a man, Tariq suggests that it may help females if they trust in themselves more. He believes women need to stress that they bring the right skills set and don't need to change to become leaders. They need to see themselves as leaders-in-waiting in order to become the type of leaders they need to be. There's often an expectation that they need to change to become more like men in order to get into those positions. However, women should hold true to the values of the different skillsets that female leaders can bring such as collaboration: listening that much more openly, being less dogmatic in approach and looking at problems in a different way from men.

Tariq recognises that it is a huge problem to reconcile this with the male perception. His hope is that one day there will be a tipping point where women's value will be recognised, leading to greater balance and equality. He does not believe it is in those males' awareness that they are cutting off or not recognising female members in their cohort, or that there is a need to bring them out in meetings, as the points they have to make are just as valuable, if not more valuable than the points that may have already been made. It's a difficult challenge to which Tariq does not believe there is one simple answer. Sometimes the structure for running boards and making decisions is focused on decision making as opposed to having discussion-based meetings. He believes there is a need for meetings to change to a more discussion based approach, which does not focus solely on making quick decisions, but allows for the exploration of the pros and cons of items in more detail. A quick, nimble approach may be perceived as great leadership, however, it's possible the organisation may be running headlong over a cliff without realising it.

Board Representation

Tariq believes that, if we don't represent our populations all the way through our organisations, we are missing the huge value of representing the population needs or having their voices heard at a senior level. If the general population of a workforce has a 50:50 gender balance, but 95% of the members of the Board are male, there is an imbalance that needs to be addressed. Such an organisation may say they believe in equality even though it's not reflected in the makeup of their board. It may reflect a blind spot in the organisation, but part of it is also a perceived threat because to create that equality, there would need to be change to how things are done. Men would have to learn to listen, collaborate and use skills that they may have been taught from a young age are not essential traits to be met to be a good leader. They will also need to eliminate some other traits. To change the structure of boards would also mean less male members on the board. This could be achieved naturally on the basis of people retiring from the board and actively looking for female replacements to balance the board representation. This does not mean discriminating in favour of women, it is about balancing a discrepancy. An alternative and perhaps less threatening approach would be to expand the board membership so the positions filled by men are held, but balanced with an equal number of female participants. Tariq can't say for sure which would be right or if there are alternative approaches that he's not aware of. As it stands, Boards typically reflect the patriarchal society that we live in and provide members with the comfort of being on boards with people they can also interact with socially. They are therefore unlikely to want to change this.

Education

Tariq believes there is some difference with younger men. However, some of the challenges in relation to gender equality stem from schooling, the structures of schools and the teaching profession. In the early years of education, where there is often more of a focus on nurturing than academic education, staffing is often female dominated with a fair number of female heads. In Secondary School education, this changes. There are more male heads and the majority of teachers teaching STEM subjects are male. Tariq believes there is an even greater discrepancy when you get to university. If you translate that to role models for young men and women as they go through the system, there is a subconscious message given that women fulfil the nurturing roles but men lead in the real world. This presents a skewed picture for both young men and women, leading to an unconsciously biased impression that sets their expectations of gendered roles in the workplace.

Tariq sees the absence of male teachers working at the nurturing level as a missing part of the equation in education and believes there's a need for more male teachers in primary education. A gender balance need to developed throughout education, highlighting great female role models in areas such as STEM subjects. Tariq further believes that every school should have a lead for equality to ensure that gender and wider equality is considered in every conversation.

Policy Change

More generally, Tariq believes that change needs to be policy driven. First and foremost parliament has to be representative of the population. If we don't have policy makers who are aware of the issues, nothing will change. If most members of parliament are men, we won't have a representation of female values that would enable the necessary changes in policy to bring about changes to education and subsequently the workforce. Tariq very much sees this as a long game that has to always be in the consciousness. He believes that, without thinking about and planning for the required change, the same conversations will be taking place in 10 years' time and nothing will have changed.

Tariq's Message to Young Females trying navigating their path:
"Be true to yourself and be yourself. Recognise the strengths within yourself, even though they are the quieter strengths. Make sure you are supported. Make sure you have your voice heard. Don't hide away or shy away. That doesn't mean shouting, but just make sure you actually express yourself. Don't forget there are lots of people out there to support you, but you need to actually ask for the support and the help, whatever that may be, whether it be advice or support from a teacher or tutor, coaching or careers advice. Seek out the support that you need to get to where you want to reach and just aim for what you are passionate about and go and do it."

Through The Years

S am Crooks was born and raised in Ireland. He came to England in 1965 to study at Cambridge before moving to Milton Keynes in 1970 as an Educational Manager at the Open University. Following a Fulbright Fellowship in America he was appointed Director of the University of London's External (International) Programme. He moved to INSEAD in France as Dean of Students & Registrar to America as European Director of the Graduate Management Admission Council. He has been a Councillor on Milton Keynes Council for over 25 years and was Mayor of Milton Keynes 2019–20.

Maturity & Confidence

While working at the Open University (OU), Sam noticed from evidence in the University's ongoing research that women appeared to demonstrate an earlier maturity than men in their ability to organise themselves, to be methodical and to balance conflicting life demands such as child care. This is echoed in observations at conventional universities where women often do better than men when there are continuous assessments throughout the year, rather than a focus on final exams. Men are, however, often more able to risk a sustained period of hectic revision before exams.

Sam also observed that if you look at tests, males tend to score better in science and technology questions; while women score better in verbal reasoning. However, if you give women longer on maths and science tests, they do just as well as men. The difference in approach of males and females, both in the class and assessments, demonstrate the requirement for good pedagogy which considers different learning styles and plays to the strengths of both males and females and more specifically individuals.

Expectations & Choices

The choices that men and women make are influenced by development, socialisations and interactions/role modelling. Things are, however, changing from how they were 50 years ago with more women now entering fields such as engineering.

Reflecting personally on his family, Sam mentions that his father was a clergyman. While his mother was qualified as a solicitor, she didn't actually work outside the home, as his father saw it as his responsibility to provide for the family even though the clergy aren't paid a high salary. This seemed to be true everywhere in the 1950s. Women rarely pursued professional jobs, except in areas such as nursing, before they got married. Once they were married, their job was typically to look after the home and the children. Reflecting back, Sam believes it was unfair to his mother, who was absolutely devoted to his father, but possibly had an unfulfilled life. Speaking to her after his father's death, he found she may not have wanted to argue cases in court, but would have enjoyed working in an organisation such as the Public Record Office. In his early days at the Open University in the 1970s, Sam came across many very capable women who built up the voluntary sector in Milton Keynes but did not pursue a professional career.

Things have changed significantly over time though; all the statistics show that the number of women in Chief Executive and Senior Management positions are creeping up. Sam believes that while the glass ceiling is clearly not broken, you can begin to see the cracks.

Confidence, Fertility & Progression

Having previously taught MBA students, Sam believes one of the challenges facing women is when their careers start. When Sam was teaching, the average MBA student was around 28 years old with about four or five years' work experience behind them by the time they took the degree. The expectation is that an MBA graduate would reach Board level in a small or medium sized company at the age of 32/33.

Sam has come across indicators from studies carried out by the Harvard Business Review over a period between 2012 and 2019, that show men are more confident than women and that male and female confidence doesn't actually merge until about 40, with male confidence subsequently declining while female confidence goes on increasing. This means that in the earlier stages of their careers, women are less confident about applying for jobs and promotions. This is not helped as women are harder on themselves when measuring their capabilities. While woman may be shy about putting themselves forward; men would not hesitate to do so. Women's fertility is also highest in their twenties to early thirties, so women also have to worry about child-bearing or risk leaving it until later, reaching senior/board level and having their first child in their mid-thirties.

Sam believes that in addition to the typical stereotypes of women, the expectation of peers also has an impact. If a woman has a group of friends with a conventional view of their role as women and mothers it is more difficult for a woman to stand out by doing something different.

From a more personal perspective, Sam has seen how things have changed from the era of his mother to his own era. Both his wife and daughter have successful professional careers, and his daughter has advanced expectations and horizons still further than those of her parents, having left Europe to graduate as a computer scientist in America.

Working with Women

Sam believes that in a working context women are often more open and empathetic than men. In his experience they are more active listeners who tend to have the ability to pick up messages in a way that men can't. In terms of the value women bring to the workplace, Sam highlights a Harvard Business Review research article: "Women Score Higher Than Men in Most Leadership Skills", by Jack Zenger and Joseph Folkman which highlights that women are rated better than men on key leadership capabilities such as taking initiative, resilience, self-development, driving for results, high integrity, development of others, inspiration of others, bold leadership, building relationships, championing change, establishing stretch goals, col-laboration and teamwork, connecting to the outside world, communication and problem solving. Men were, however, shown as better at developing a strategy within a business environment.

Sam has also noticed that women are very good at setting parameters with teams. Staff like to know the details of what they are meant to do, and the required standards. Where men may give a quick message, women are more inclined to sit down with the team and give greater clarity about the likes of expectations and timeframes.

Women's Historical Roles

Sam recollects some very capable women that he worked with who were unquestionably just as able as men. He remembers the 70s and early 80s when there were a lot of women working for men as secretaries before desktop computers became common. There were few expectations of the "girls" in the office. They were often young and the stereotype expectation was that if they weren't already married, they would soon get married and become pregnant and that's all they really wanted. Work structures largely defined by gender, were paralleled by the typical structure in homes. People played to those roles in line with their peer groups. This went on to reinforce expectations people had of both others and themselves based on gender.

Women working as secretaries or in the typing pool rarely seemed to aspire to work beyond this level. At that time, however, you wouldn't have found a university graduate working in the typing pool, though this could happen in equivalent roles now. Class was also a factor that came to play to impact on expectations. Sam is now retired so he can't say how embedded these structures remain in the workplace. He does, however, know that there is still a problem with salaries based on gender and thinks this may reflect the biases that remain within the work structure.

Greater Balance & Improvements

Sam believes that one improvement for women is that they are now better able to have a career and to manage it in parallel with raising a family, due to the improving provision for maternity, paternity and parental leave. The expectation that a man should always be the provider has also changed. The issues with gender pay equity were recently highlighted via the BBC pay disputes. Until very recently there was still a gender disparity in prize money in sports tournaments such as Tennis, though there is now a beginning of a coming together. Language is also changing as people are less inclined to refer to younger women at work as girls or dollybirds. They are also more likely to say please can you 'staff' the reception desk, rather than 'man' the reception desk. There's a move to saying 'human-kind', rather than 'mankind' and more reference now to 'partners' rather than 'husbands' or 'wives'. Sam believes the language we use is very important.

Further Change

Sam believes there is still a need for further change. We need to look at each career and find ways of giving women confidence to be able to take a break in their careers without it affecting them. This might mean doing anything that we can safely do to lengthen the fertility period so they can pursue their career to a senior level without feeling that there is a risk of trying to have children at too late an age. There needs to be a better balance between careers, fertility and safety. All of this needs to be considered on a career by career basis because it will be different in various careers.

Sam doesn't believe that women's progression disadvantages men, but sees it as one of the healthiest things that could have happened. He explains that if you want to have a liberal democratic society, there has to be the ability to exercise freedom of choice. If you want to exercise freedom of choice, it has to be a true freedom, which means that women must have the economic strength to exercise the freedoms of choice that men already have. That's why he believes it's so important to try to establish true equality. If it means that men lose out temporarily until there is equality, then so be it.

His recommendation to young women, is to do their own thing. There will be people to back them, whatever they decide to do.

Systemic Change

C hris Gillies has extensive experience working at Senior Executive level in top firms in Financial Services. With over 40 years' experience in business, he has also spent a fair amount of time volunteering for various charities for the past 30 years. He now works as a Non-Executive Director, Mentor and Advisor and is on the Board of several charities.

The Theology of Gender and Women in Leadership

As a Christian, when the Church was grappling with the role of women in Church and whether women should be allowed to lead and have a voice, Chris did quite a lot of theological study on the subject in order to understand the challenge. He found for every one verse in the Bible that indicated a problem with women in leadership, there were at least 10 affirming verses that said the opposite. There is so much in scripture and theology that shows that women are equally valued by God as leaders as men. As a result, Chris is convinced that as women have led in the past they can lead today, bringing important perspectives and the capability to bring anointed leadership. This theological belief underpins Chris' thinking in his business practice.

Chris notes that the three people he mentors in the non-profit sector at the moment are all women. He's mentored women throughout his career, without specifically focusing on gender. It's just been that they've approached him and asked him. In turn, he has had the opportunity to learn from them and increase his level of understanding.

Responsible Business

Working with Allied Dunbar, and then Zurich Insurance Group, which are both financial organisations that very much wanted to do the right thing, a key focus during Chris' career has been on responsible business. Chris' initial involvement in charity was partly due to the organisation encouraging staff to volunteer for charity.

There was a very positive moral environment in Allied Dunbar's Head Office, with a need to ensure that the field sales operation was aligned to this. This led to the design of products that were safer, more suitable, better value for money and transparent. Being involved in this in the 1990s gave Chris the enthusiasm to continue the work to develop responsible business when he worked for Zurich Insurance, extending beyond external facing areas and challenges including: products, business realignment and an ethical investment strategy for internal challenges such as executive pay and incentive schemes, gender with a focus on the fairness of women's pay, the fairness of recruitment policies to women, and the opportunities available to women for advancement.

Pressure Points

Thinking in general terms, Chris agrees that there are problems in relation to women's pay, recruitment and advancement, and he focuses on these key pressure points that have a major impact on women.

Recruitment

At a basic level, Chris speaks of the recruitment process and the challenge of persuading people to look at a balanced shortlist of candidates comprising three men and three women, all of whom can do the job. Chris finds that even this can be a challenge for some organisations. In his experience, if you are able to create an open process that delivers a balanced shortlist and then aim to hire the best person for the job, you've already done something that will dramatically increase women's chances of being appointed.

Chris believes there is also a need to be aware that at the level of middle and senior management positions, men naturally tend to have more experience than most women, as they generally haven't taken time off to have children. If you go one step further and recognise that diverse teams tend to be more resilient, more creative, and more able to solve problems, then Chris believes that you can make another mindset change. It's not so much about hiring the best person for the job, but rather thinking about hiring the best person for the team. Considering the perspective: 'I've got five men and one woman in my team. If I hired another woman, that would work wonders for the balance in my team and give additional support to that solitary female who may be struggling to find an ally.' Ultimately, thinking about the team's diversity, creativity and lived experience might lead to a different choice than if you just hired the best person for that particular post. Chris does not see this as positive discrimination, but as working to try to be balanced: recruiting to bring out additional synergy in a team.

Pay

Chris mentions that a lot of research demonstrates that women tend to thank their prospective employer and accept the first pay offer made during recruitment, while men have a tendency to negotiate for more. This means that women tend to start on lower salaries than men. The problems with the Gender Pay Gap therefore start from when people are hired, with women often starting off being paid around 5% less than men with the same job and ability. Other things being equal, this then feeds further inequality into the system that becomes increas-ingly difficult to put right later. Some people would say that women are responsible for this situation because they should have more con-fidence in their ability and ask for more, which would lead to them being paid the same as men. Chris believes there is an argument that hiring managers are responsible for trying to pay what they can get away with, rather than what the person or job is really worth;   at times this goes as far as opting for the candidate who might be willing to accept less when it comes to a final decision over two candidates with similar abilities. Chris also believes that Milton Friedman's views have led to a system that focuses too heavily on corporate profit-ability, which has contributed to this approach to pay.

Progression

Another critical factor that Chris noticed in financial services is that there tends to be a 50:50 gender split at junior levels, at times even a 60:40 female to male split. However, the number of females at middle management level is much reduced and by the time you reach senior levels there is typically an 80:20 male to female gender split. Chris believes this is partly because of the different life choices that a lot of women make, contrasted to what is required to reach more senior positions; with not every women willing or able to do the things which may be required, such as working long hours with a focus on power, status and success at the expense of family and a more balanced lifestyle.

Chris believes there is also employers' bias against women taking career breaks to go on maternity leave, causing career interruptions. Even in modern firms where men may go on paternity leave for two weeks when they have a child, this just amounts to a holiday, whilst a woman on maternity leave is absent for several months or longer. Men also don't tend to experience issues such as postpartum depression. As a result, there can be a window of about ten years in women's lives where their careers are hugely interrupted, if you assume women having two or three children over that period.

If employers took a sufficiently farsighted view, they would realise that if they stick by women during that ten year period, there's likely to be another 20 to 30 years on the other side where women can be some of the most loyal, productive and focused employees of all. A number of employers let such women fall by the wayside instead of building systems and processes to help re-engage women by letting them make the life choices they feel they need to make, staying in touch with them while on maternity leave, and providing them with flexible working patterns on their return. As a result, the environment can be fairly hostile to mums.

Succession Planning

Chris summarises that all the problems he has already highlighted make it difficult for succession planning that gets enough women to the really top executive positions in business where there are currently very few women.

There is nothing that Chris says that is meant as negative towards women and what he says reflects general trends that he has observed in many different organisations. More than anything it is the system that needs to change to benefit; however, we are talking of a patriarchy system which has existed for over 5000 years old. Chris explains that the last 100-150 years of Management Science have been focused on productivity and how you do more for lower costs. The relentless focus on productivity has a spin-off of valuing people who work long and hard without realising this may gradually lower productivity over time. As a result, the focus is typically on the short term without realising the long term damage the system causes.

The Experience of Working With Women

Over time, Chris has learnt different perspectives from working women, both those who have reported to him and those who have worked alongside him. He finds that women often tend to have different perspectives from men and are often more insightful. This, together with an understanding of their experiences when they are prepared to be open with him, taught him to fully value women and to proactively have more women on his teams so that there are more diverse voices in the room. He mentions that this extends to diversity far beyond just the employment of women. He is ultimately looking for better performance as a result of greater diversity of thought and lived experience.

Chris also recognises the additional challenges that women from minority backgrounds are likely to face in trying to navigate what is often a white male dominated environment. He does not for one minute believe they are less effective, bring less to the party, or are of lower value. They also bring different perspectives which help to create more resilience, diversity and creativity in the team provided you are willing to give them a voice.

Easing the Journey for Women

For women's journeys to be easier, Chris suggests that women be strong without being strident and more confident in their ability and worth. He believes that finding positive female role models to inspire women in the workplace is critical. He also recommends enlisting the help and support of supportive men. To this end, Chris highlights the importance of Women's Innovation Networks to support women. In his corporate experience, such networks tended to get additional traction when a few men are invited to meetings to speak or just affirm what is happening within the network. He has observed that when a few senior men come to such events, giving a talk or just sitting in the front row to listen and join in the networking, more men want to be involved and support the activities, almost as a badge of honour. Crucial though, is to invite men who have a valuable perspective to bring.

For women trying to navigate the work environment, Chris

believes it takes heart to navigate the work environment. There has been enormous change and progress over the last 50 years, but women should continue to speak out against injustice because it's still widespread. Women may not be able to have it all, but if they make intelligent trade-offs, they can be successful in their work. Women should find men who are willing to be supportive and make such men their allies.

Most especially to young women, Chris says directly, "Never stop learning. Set yourself high standards: be ethical, enthusiastic, loyal and reliable, because attitude speaks louder than gender." Also note that "Poor managers can teach you as much as good managers because they teach you how not to manage."

Intentionality

B ill Palmer is an Executive Coach based in the
San Fransisco Bay area of the US with global
experience. He links business results to corporate
culture and process, with attention to individual action,
integrity and transformation. Bill brings the challenges
of Diversity, Equity and Inclusion to all of his work.

Intentionality

Bill grew up in a Jewish family and so he was not unaware of discrimination and prejudice growing up. His parents were moral people
who taught him integrity, principles and ethics. He doesn't see himself as having anything personal to gain, however, he would like to
see his country being in line with its ideals as opposed to being out of
line with them.

In introducing himself, Bill explains that as an Executive and
Leadership Coach, he has specialised, although not exclusively, in the
areas of Diversity, Equity and Inclusion. This means he brings this to
every single piece of work he does. Bill believes, if Diversity, Equity

and Inclusion are not part of his coaching he's not doing a full job as a coach. Sometimes people are surprised by this, sometimes annoyed, as in their minds they simply want to be better leaders and don't understand the relevance of speaking specifically about women, African-Americans or other areas of diversity. It's not Bill's only emphasis, however, it's one thing that differentiates him from a number of his colleagues.

The Value of Women at Work

Bill's belief in inclusion naturally leads to a question about the value that women bring to the workplace that would actually encourage the people he works with to want to include them. As Bill points out, as women make up at least half of the population, it is quite hard to generalise. However to stereotype on the basis of the women that he has dealt with in the workplace, he explains women are more attentive to process than many men and are generally less attached to outcomes. He adds that they seem in general, though not always, to better manage what he would call the soft side of the business world i.e. communication skills, people skills, creating common ground and things like that. Bill emphasises that these are all gross generalisations, but he would stand by them to a great extent. He has, however, met women who are as vicious, competitive and as cutthroat as men can be. He's also met men who are process-oriented and engage in soft skills.

Bitches and Bimbos

Because of the obstacles placed in the way of women, Bill believes they tend to have a different perspective from the mostly male people who have put those obstacles in their way and this presents a valuable perspective. Bill explains that the same behaviour that gets men identified as forceful, dramatic, charismatic, intelligent good leaders gets women identified as 'bitches'. The same behaviour that would get a man identified as social, friendly, warm, engaging, nice, fun person would get many women identified as 'bimbos'. That is an obstacle that's placed in women's way which to a great extent is built into our culture.

Hierarchal Numbers

Bill also speaks of numbers. If you look at a hierarchal organisation, which reflects the organisation structure of most organisations, it's a pyramid. As you get closer to the top, there's less and less room for people. As a result, in a game where the rules are stacked against a particular group, the likelihood is that women will not be able to play the game well enough to get towards the top. The people who have organised the game and who have set the rules are more able to play to win.

Unhelpful Behaviours

When it comes to obstacles that women may create for themselves, Bill says there are certain behaviours that women have been trained to engage in, which they need to unlearn and learn new ones which will help them to get where they want to go. To illustrate this Bill speaks of a workshop about "Bitches and Bimbos" which he ran for a group of female employees.

During the workshop, he put clips of films into two categories. The first category was videos which showed classically witchy or bitchy women behaviours such as a scene from *The Wizard of Oz* where the Wicked Witch of the West is a terribly mean and evil character who says she's going to get Dorothy and do terrible things to her. He also includes a clip from *The Devil Wears Prada* in which Meryl Streep plays a boss who dissects and destroys her female assistant, played by Anne Hathaway. For the second category, Bill took clips that demonstrated what is seen as bimbo type of behaviours such as the clip of Marilyn Monroe singing Happy Birthday to President Kennedy, together with other clips in which the female character would typically be described as "dumb blondes".

During the workshop the group spoke of the typical character-isations of each group. The first group are bitchy, nasty and mean. Not stopping there, Bill went on to ask about the positive qualities of these characters to which was added that both were factually correct, quite forceful and clear, speaking with power and giving directions. With the 'bimbo' type of characters, even though they are typically classified as dumb, stupid, idiots, on the positive side they are warm, friendly, open, sociable and kind.

Focusing the positive sides to the characters in each group, the proposition was then put to the women in the room that they can be forceful, directing, clear and factually correct without acting in a manner which would lead them to be classified as bitchy. Similarly they can be sociable, friendly, warm and connected without being seen as idiotic, dumb or stupid.

Bill further expands, the obstacles that some women place in their own way include buying into these stereotypes without examin-ing them and saying what are the positive qualities that they, as an individual, want to take on. By discussing cases of how they had pre-viously acted within certain situations the women on the workshop were able to better understand their behaviour in the past and to determine how they could do things more positively in the future.

On the other hand, there are some women who simply adopt what Bill refers to as traditional male, capitalist values and just try to become like men. It's more difficult to help them; most especially as they may get promoted or achieve some positive outcomes and results, leading to the thinking that their behaviours are effective.

Metrics & Quotas

Discussing what needs to change within the system, Bill speaks of the need for the use of metrics in organisations in the private sector, non-profits or government organisations. Organisations need to think of measurements/metrics on areas such as the percentage of women in the workforce, the percentage of senior leadership which is female, African-Americans or the inclusion of other minority groups in the organisation. If the percentages show a bias, then things need to be done to correct the imbalances over time.

Bill recognises that some people hate to hear it, but he believes quotas are a solution in relation to both race and gender. The quotas don't have to be directly in line with population demographics, but they should lead to representation which better reflects reality. Bill doesn't believe it's right or good when there is under representation. All the studies that he has seen show that when workforces are diverse they are healthier and it leads to better results. There are structural problems that need to change to allow for a fairer system.

To the counter argument that people often use, saying that they simply go for the most qualified people, Bill responds that he would agree if they are able to assess the most qualified without bias. To the argument people make saying they'd don't see gender or colour, Bill responds that this amounts to a confession of blindness. If people claim to be objective on this basis, it's often a reflection of bias as no one is truly objective; bias is built into us. It's most dangerous when we don't recognise that we have a bias. On the other hand, if we recognise that we have a bias, we can set up systems of checks and balances to make sure that their effect is minimal. Through 360 degree feedback, Bill has been able to awaken people to the reality that in spite of their perception they may have favourites and are not always as fair as they may have believed.

Blind Auditions & Applications

Bill tells the story of Cincinnati Symphony Orchestra in the 1950s. At this point in time, 95% of the people in Symphony Orchestras in America were men. The leader of the Cincinnati Symphony Orchestra instituted the practice of blind auditions in which auditioners selecting performers would listen to the person auditioning play their instrument behind a curtain so that the auditionee could not be seen. They were additionally asked to take their shoes off so that women wearing high heels could not be identifies by the distinctive sound of their heels. This practice has now spread all over the symphony orchestra world of the United States. The Symphony Orchestra world in the US is still not 50-50, but it's close. Bill believes a similar approach can be taken to Recruitment and Hiring as a lot of organisations have started to do. He gives the example of a client's organisation in which one person makes the final call on hiring a person, however, gender and race have been blanked out from resumes. Bill additionally refers to a famous study that showed that if the name on your resume was Kamau, with the exact same qualifications you got many fewer call-backs than if your name was Kenneth. As a result many organisations have made changes whereby people are hired based on qualifications.

Less Positive Men

Bill believes that among men, there's an irreducible core of men who mistreat and hate women who will never change. Asked why, Bill explains that he believes such men feel threatened or reflect what they were taught growing up living in an environment where women were subservient and catered to men, where the model of masculinity was powerful, strong, uncompromising, tough and in command of women. Such experiences affect how they respond to women within the work environment.

More Positive Men

For the male leader who is open to idea of females in his organisation and to their advance who does not know how to navigate this, Bill recommends that he starts by first speaking to the men in his organisation about what he wants to achieve and what they can do generally to support women. The first step is to shut down the sniggers and suggestive remarks that many men make to each other about women behind their backs. A leader with hierarchal authority can tell both direct reports and peers that this is not acceptable. They basically need to set the norms about how they want a team to work together, including how they cooperate, collaborate, create and work hard, as well as the norms as to how men and women treat each other within the organisation. He emphasises that they can and should set the norms.

Women – Navigating and Progressing

For women trying to navigate into and upwards within organisations, Bill recommends that they develop the skills of creating alliances and networks. If you're in a game where the rules are stacked against you and you're the underdog then one of the avenues that is open to you is to leverage the power of connection by not being a solo pilot. This can be achieved by creating relationships between men and women that are supportive; where the support is mutual. Most organisations are intensely political, so the ticket of admission for advancement is at least some form of competence where it is subject matter expertise and knowing what you're doing so that people can recognise you for it. After that it's politics. Politics may be seen as a dirty word, but it is how people advance and get to the top. It doesn't mean being cynical or phoney; or using relationships in a way that's completely selfish, but by making connections and building alliances. Legislation gets through Parliament or Congress because it serves the need of a majority of the people voting on it. As such, if a woman is Vice President in an organisation and wants to be Senior Vice President, she's not going to get there solely on her own merit (or as a man would do). She's going to get there because she has accumulated enough political capital, enough retail capital to cash in to get the job. There are men as well as women that don't understand the need to manage relationships in order to advance. Many times, because women are often in the minority in terms of the corporate structure, they feel isolated and try to fly solo and try to stand out purely because of their work. This handicaps them as it's like fighting with one hand tied behind your back.

The Responsibility of Men

In concluding, Bill emphasises that a lot of the work that needs to be done, needs to be done by men. He believes it's wrong to ask women to sort out men's sexist attitudes. Men can do a lot at an individual level to make sure that their attitudes, behaviours and beliefs are supportive of women generally, not just in their workplace, but supportive of a fair, equitable and just organisational world of work. Outside of that irreducible core of men that will never change, there's a large number of men who are of goodwill. They don't need to be hit over the head. They just need to understand that the impact of their behaviour is at times different from their actual intent.

Catalysts to Change

Tarro Morris is the Capability Manager with responsibility for Learning & Development for Production at Carlsberg Group in Northampton, England. Tarro has worked for Carlsberg for over 14 years, having previously worked in the Automotive Industry.

Carlsberg Apprenticeship Scheme

Tarro's initial reaction to the question around the Value of Women at Work is sadness that it is even arises as a topic for discussion. Over the last couple of years, he has led on the recruitment of three apprenticeships for Carlsberg's Production Department, which is a very male dominated part of the organisation. With a focus on getting the best people for the job, they have recruited a young man and two young women, one of whom was born in England and the other in Iran. While recognising that the young man who had started at a later stage than the young women, came with his own skills and value to the organisation, we focused our conversation on the young women who Tarro finds to be very vocal about their opinions, inquisitive and thought provoking. They have the tendency to spend time observing what the experienced workers do, ask questions for clarification and then try to do things themselves. Tarro finds it quite enlightening that they don't constantly seek reassurance as he did when he was young.

When Carlsberg decided to start an apprenticeship programme in 2018 with Tarro as lead, they partnered with Milton Keynes College as their provider. They were very specific that anyone interested in one of the positions needs to apply to the College and not contact the organisation directly. As there is a lot of intergenerational male employment in the organisation meaning there may be grandfathers, fathers and sons all working together, Carlsberg wanted a more open process whereby they were able to direct anyone interested in applying to the College, with the College providing a shortlist of candidates. With this process, Carlsberg only knew the first names of candidates when they came for the assessment day. This meant that family members of existing members of staff could apply (a way of passing skills down from one generation to the next). However it removed the risk of concerns over nepotism and created the awareness that every-one has a fair chance of getting a job with the organisation regardless of whether they have a relative working there.

Female Influences

One of Tarro's greatest female influences is his wife, whom he has been with since he was sixteen. He went out to work from the age of eighteen wanting to be a provider while his wife did her A levels and went on to do a degree in Psychology while also working. She went on to become a teacher and has now progressed to become the Head Teacher of an Infant School. Tarro also speaks very proudly of his two daughters.

Tarro has also worked with some great women, some of whom he calls friends. He highlights the example of a Manager named Karen King who used to work at Carlsberg. She was a good influence on him, who mentored and nurtured him in the role that he is now in. She also helped him to feel confident and empowered in his role.

The Impact of the Female Apprentices

A key value that he has found in the women he's worked with is that he very much appreciates is their openness and honesty. He finds that they tend to challenge with a clear purpose about things they've thought through, and you feel as if there is less of an agenda when they are talking to you. As demonstrated in production, men tend to do things based on how they've done things in the past, whereas the women (even the apprentices they now have) tend to consider the current process and suggest alternative options. In production he has found that the women are less 'gung ho' and have a more tempered approach, not rushing to complete products, but slowing things down at times in order to think about what they are doing and why they are doing them. Doing so in the production department is leading the men to stop to listen and think through the processes themselves. Tarro has recognised that besides the diversity the women add to the team; their approach may also be partly down to their youth, so it's perhaps a modern way of thinking. Ultimately, it adds a freshness and richness to the process.

Reflecting on why there were previously no women in the production team, Tarro doesn't believe this is so much because the opportunities for them were not there, but because women didn't apply for the roles.

Currently, Carlsberg is only running engineering apprenticeships but in the future they hope to branch out more into other parts of the organisation.

Tarro believes that the presence of females such as the two apprentices working for Carlsberg will encourage other females to apply for roles in such organisations. One of the female apprentices has been approached by an organisation about the possibility of becoming a mentor to other females. The last time he presented to prospective apprentices at the College, one of the young women went with him and he was able to refer to her as a young woman who had successfully taken on an apprenticeship so that people could see that it wasn't just for men. Tarro hopes that in a few years' times, the current apprentices will be confident enough to do the presentations for future recruitment rounds. By this time they would be successful engineers giving the message that, "I can do it, you can do it too". He hopes this will give people the encouragement to apply with the knowledge that there will be people around to support them. Tarro believes that the courses available via the College have also helped attract a diversity of candidates.

Tarro has been pleased that the older generation of engineers in the company don't really see them as young women, to be treated differently, but as people to teach how to do things properly and pass their knowledge on. In the process, they have improved the manner in which they actually do things, ensuring they themselves follow proper process. It has also meant that the men have become more conscious of the language they use at work, considering what they're saying and why they are actually saying it. As a result they have become more thoughtful. Also on the positive side, the women seem to be totally comfortable sitting with the men at lunch and interacting freely with them. All of this means there is much less nervousness or concern about bringing more women into the teams in the future.

Message to Young Females

For a young female starting their career, Tarro's recommendation is that she be herself; there will a position somewhere that is right for her. She shouldn't feel the need to change who she is because she feels it's necessary to do so; the right people will always be successful.

As he always says to his daughters: "Make sure you're doing things because you want to and not because you think it's right for somebody else or you'll never enjoy it. Have friendships with people who will help mentor you and draw you towards the right sort of people. You'll always come across people who don't like you, it's how you deal with those people to strive forward to be able to put a better version of yourself forward. Don't be baited. If you come across the wrong sort of behaviour or attitude, feel confident to say something at the time, but if you don't feel confident to do so, do what feels safe and right for you at the time, even if it means walking away and speaking to a person who is going to help you in the right sort of way. So find coaches, mentors and friends."

A Board Level View – Push

———

Thomas Power is a Chairman, Board Member and Advisor to several organisations. He also runs Mastermind Groups with his wife, Penny Power OBE. In addition, he is a Social Media Personal Branding Specialist, Social Influencer, Published Author and Professional Speaker.

A lot of Thomas's success comes from his ability to access and follow what is going on within the business environment and beyond; connect with people and develop and support new innovations.

The Sophistication of a Woman

Thomas sees women as more sophisticated in their approach than men. Men are very focused on precise results and typically believe businesses are about numbers such as profit numbers, sales numbers and sales price numbers. This is often the focus within board meetings. While numbers are important, Thomas finds women tend to focus more on the overall business: the community, the ecosystem, and the 'bits' around the edge. Women tend to take a more peripheral view while men tend to look straight ahead.

Thomas doesn't believe one is better than the other, as you need both. Even though women in their approach may seem complicated and hard for men to understand, both approaches are necessary. Thomas believe men are quite basic to understand, while with women there is a sophistication with so many parts to decipher that makes them complicated. He believes for men to better understand women, mothers need to teach their sons more about women when they are little.

Women on Boards

Thomas enjoys working with women. In general terms, while men may make better engineers, women make better marketers or sales people. This is not to say you can't have good female engineers or good male sales people. However, based on his real life experience of working on twenty different Boards over a 30 year period, when it comes to Boards he would typically lead women towards roles in areas such as Sales, Marketing, Human Supports, Customer Services and Quality. Asked if this could be seen as stereotyping, Thomas explains that he's been working for 40 years since he was 16 and this is what his experience has taught him. It's not to say that men and women can't have other skills, but he has noticed a natural leaning.

Push

Speaking on the fact that there's still a minority of women at the Board level with all the value that he identifies women bring, Thomas expresses the concern that women rarely come across as competitive or ambitious enough to push for a seat on Boards. In his experience, Boards are not anti-female or prejudiced in general. There are some very skilled women who he thinks should be on Boards who do not ask. It's unusual to be invited on a Board unless you're an international superstar brand type of personality. You generally have to push to get on a Board. Men tend to push, women don't.

Women who want to be on Boards need to get the right type of qualifications for the type of Board they want to be on and push. You need the right qualifications: a personal brand online, to be known as a person who can sit on a board, but you are selected through networking. Networking may range from activities such as golf, football, rugby, drinking and partying. Men are more transactional in this manner, while women are less inclined to do these things in order to achieve the outcomes. It's a male type of networking, however, as things stand, Boards are predominantly male, even in organisations that are more female-orientated such as in creative organisations.

Men are more likely to get involved in a female network and push for what they want. Women tend to feel less comfortable pushing their way into a male network for all sorts of reasons, which are not necessarily positive. Sometimes male networks can feel threatening, predatory or political. Women don't typically play the networking games that men play. In reality, it's like software. The system may not be well designed, but you still have to learn how to use it.

Diversity on Boards in Reality

While Thomas agrees that it is possible that organisations have a responsibility to change their systems to be more gender-neutral, so that they can realise the benefits of females on their Boards, in reality,

Thomas doesn't believe companies would actually know how to do this.

Thomas believes it is important for Boards to be diverse, not just in terms of gender, but also in terms of other characteristics such as colour, race, sexual orientation and religion. If invited to a Board which was predominantly male, he'd suggest they ask someone else.

In reality, unless you've got all the right skills at the boardroom table, you won't be able to serve the market as you'll miss out certain sections of the market and in particular cities. For global organisations, there is a need to have a representation of big cities such as London, New York and San Francisco where big deals tend to happen. It's where the big money is. There is a need to have a broadly based Board to service complex markets.

Thomas thinks having female board members is important, as are other areas of diversity such as race and sexual orientation. However, there are different regulations in different countries which may affect areas such as the number of board members. A lot of Boards tend to have three executive members from within the company and four independent non-executives. For organisations with products for a global market, there is a tendency to have one from Europe, one from North America, one from Asia and one from Africa depending on the markets being served. Thomas believes when you consider the geographical requirements for Board members, it becomes more difficult to consider all the other areas of diversity such as gender unless people intersect across different diversity strands. The specific selection of females needs to therefore be on the basis of the markets that they are targeting. Women need to have the market and product experience. An additional benefit would be a geographical connection to the market(s) being targeted.

Thomas agrees it may be of value to review and increase the number of Board members; however, they are currently determined by the Financial Conduct Authority in each market. Even with larger companies where you have Boards across different regions, you can still only have so many people at board meetings or you wouldn't get anything done.

Inspiring Women

It's no surprise that the woman in business that Thomas finds most inspiring is his wife, Penny. He describes her as an incredible listener and a fantastic coach. "She's great at listening and then getting people to a place of doing things they really want to do.", he says. Thomas on the other hand sees himself as the better mentor as he directs and tells people what they need to do and then waits for them to do it. He believes they complement each other in this way.

Thomas is also inspired and very impressed by the Kardashian family. He explains that they have built a multi-billion dollar Empire from nothing. Anyone who can turn ideas into capital is a true alchemist as far as Thomas is concerned. The Kardashian mother and daughters have used their ideas to create a female Empire. Some people may focus on their looks, however, they have used their ideas to create a multi-billion dollar empire. There's also Beyonce. There aren't many female entrepreneurs at that level who stand out to Thomas as such he notices the likes of the Kardashians and Beyonce when he sees them. Thomas refers back to his concern that women rarely push enough. The Kardashian's push their ideas out there, he says. They've got a range of products and brands inclusive of cosmetics, clothing, music-related products, software, television and media and content products. They are good with what they do, but they also push.

Contextualising Pushing

Thomas say's his wife, Penny on the other hand doesn't push, but has a very gentle approach. She is successful without pushing. However to get on Boards there is a need for women to push more. In addition to having the right skills; they have to network in the places where people are considering people for such position. This often means men's networks. However, female candidates are rarely available at such networks to be chosen from when choices for boards are being made.

Thomas did a quick online search for Board member on both LinkedIn or Twitter. The majority of people that come up on both networks are men. From the LinkedIn search, eight out of ten of the first ten people that came up were men. Women need to be more visible; that is what Thomas says he means by pushing. It's not that women don't have the skills, capabilities and interest, but they are not going to those networks or putting the words in their online profiles that would make them come up in a search. Women need to be visible both offline and online. In addition to the men's networks, there are plenty of female networks and more mixed networks. Thomas believes if you want things you must network. If you want information, contacts, deals, Board seats this usually comes from networking more than marketing and social media. In Thomas's experience, people want the best person, but that person has to be visible to them. If you don't turn up for the interview, i.e. have a presence, you will not be chosen.

Quotas

Thomas doesn't believe the idea of quotas to increase gender diversity on Boards is a bad idea. He doesn't however, believe it's in tune with the market as it can be perceived as bureaucratic, preventing people from searching where they would naturally want to search to find people.

To a Young Woman

For a young woman starting out in her career who wants to rise to senior levels of organisations, Thomas would recommend that she develop a well-rounded knowledge in the different parts of the organisation they are working for, understanding its products and services, the industry they are in and the wider market. They should also develop their networking skills and learn to navigate. He believes there is also a need to develop a level of sophisticated, gentle persuasion.

Thomas believes women also need to believe in their own ideas and not simply take other people's ideas as gospel. They need to develop their own brand which needs to be reviewed and renewed on a regular basis, constantly reinventing themselves to be able to survive in constantly changing markets.

Mindset

Ryan Kelly is a serial entrepreneur from the South Eastern part of the United States of America. He runs a number of organisations inclusive of Othal Partners, a full service niche-marking, events creation and management organisation; Port-of-Go and exclusive business travel and tourism service, and the Opal Network Alliance, which runs the Central Florida Women's Summit and other corporate events for women.

Context

Ryan believes that the intrinsic values and societal/cultural beliefs that we grow up with, good, bad or indifferent, become the modus operandi for the way business operates. Ryan probably has more women than men in his network and with a daughter and grand-daughter, he wants to see women treated equally with men. He wants them to be the best version of themselves and reach their fullest potential without anyone putting a glass ceiling in the way to create a barrier for them. He believes the glass ceiling is a reality, you just try to break the ice in different situations and mitigate it so things gets a little easier. While he's not dogmatic or chauvinistic, Ryan does not believe in the form of feminism that creates the impression that men are not needed, believing that men and women are of equal value.

Opal Network Alliance

This is clear by the fact that Ryan runs the Opal Network Alliance (ONA) which has been running multicultural seminars and career fairs for women since 2011. Ryan wanted to use the events to support people who have been historically and irrefutably disenfranchised from the process of becoming successful. Women are a key group of people in this category, most especially women of colour i.e. black, Hispanic or Asian women who typically have an even tougher time.

Covering a number of the challenges that women face on a day-to-day basis, the ONA programmes cover a number of modules such as understanding multiculturalism in a way that goes beyond just looking at our differences, but also having the dialogue that enables us to build connections among people based on our commonalities.

The programmes also cover areas of communication such as Social Media, Public Speaking, Business Etiquette and Business Development focusing on being able to reinvent yourself because of changes to careers which may occur because of the Corona Virus Pandemic. This leads into areas of entrepreneurship such as business development and growth, seed funding and networking. Networking is crucial, as it's possible that a woman could be in a room with decision makers, but feel too shy or unable to approach them. The programmes also go as far as covering areas such as Legal Rights, Parenting and Nutrition and Health amongst other things.

Ryan also works to address the challenges with corporations of being male dominated with very few females at a senior level. This is addressed through a programme: 'Connecting Men and Progressing Women' with the goal of engaging people and ultimately creating a sense of belonging where everyone believes they have a vested interest in the organisation they work for because they are valued and listened to, being made to feel important.

Challenges in the Workplace

On the challenges that women are faced with in the workplace, Ryan believes that the same old adage of sexism often still comes to play, whereby women are viewed based on how they dress and look, how young or old they are before anything else, occurring most especially in male dominated offices. In such environments there is often more of an interest in appearance and what women add to the office aesthetics than expertise and qualifications. They may not say this in public, though there is a tendency for some men to say it to each other. Women on their own part don't always support other women and rather see them as competitors.

Ryan believes these factors combine to mean women are not always fully valued or given the opportunity to contribute in the workplace to the full extent of their abilities. This often leaves women feeling under-utilised and unhappy with a number of them ending up leaving their jobs. It is a key reason why Ryan advocates entrepreneurship as an option for women to be able demonstrate their capabilities.

Working with Women

Ryan actually finds women a lot easier to work with then men, as there tends to be a lot less bravado and egotism. In his experience, he has also found that they focus in on getting things done when a request is made. As a result, he currently works in collaboration with seven different consultants of which five are women and only two are men. He's found women to bring a certain attitude, tending to be innately passionate and more nurturing about any project they take on, cuddling it like a baby. They think things through in detail and take a very skilful approach to what needs to be done. This, Ryan acknowledges, does not apply to all women, but he has come across many women and it is key to why he is particularly interested in investing in women from a wide diversity of backgrounds.

Ryan believes that while business owners like himself see the value of women, having grown up in a society that disenfranchises them regardless of how good they are. This has led a number of women to start their own businesses. They often start off in their homes and develop into success stories from there. He believes they do not always assert themselves enough though. He further believes it's almost biblical to say that if women do learn to assert themselves and keep knocking at the door, someone will eventually open it and provide them with everything they need to help get the success they want. He believes there is therefore a need for women to assert themselves and not be intimidated by tradition, men's demeanour or how long they may have been in their position. It's important for women to learn to talk to the managers, but not pester them when there is a chance to do so and to take time to talk to them about the projects they may be working on and improvements and solutions to the way things work; making them aware of what they are capable of. This may also mean going the extra mile such that when A and B is required, they go on to do C and D to ensure that the woman's value is recognised and optimised so that she can have the success that she wants rather than just have a job.

Organisations Limits without Women

Ryan believes that if an organisation or team is built solely on the capabilities of men there will be a limit to its success, no matter how successful it appears. If the world's greatest resource is people, but a certain segment of society has been left out, how can it really be said that organisation or team is doing its best to optimise and better itself? How can it be most productive? Ryan believes there is a need for this self-evaluation to take place. When women are engaged, they need to be engaged differently than what has historically been done across most of the globe. In the modern work environment, there is a need to think globally and be aware of future trends. The key to achieving this is through the inclusion of staff at every level within the operation. The programme that Ryan runs on 'Connecting Men and Progressing Women' has a focus on encouraging greater dialogue through panel discussions on how to include and advance women. Ryan believes there is a strong need to involve men in the advancement of women as it can't just be down to women; we all need to work together with a slightly different approach to the overall goals of corporations. Men have a vital part to play in a transition through advisory councils and committees to help companies to start to grow and flourish in different ways so that an organisation becomes the think tank it is supposed to be with no discrimination. In this transition, Ryan believes it is important to ensuring the inclusion of women of colour who are often conspicuously absent and have a different set of challenges from white women.

Cultural Differences

Ryan believes that it is often the case that after work, while a white woman may go back to her home in the suburbs, the black woman not hired will be struggling, possibly on welfare, impoverished with her children not doing very well in school, because she doesn't have the socio-economic status that will help her do better for herself as the system as a whole discriminates against your skin colour.

Focusing on the American South, Ryan says the difference in perception of black and white women and their roles extends to the workplace due to our intrinsic socialisation. There is a different mental attitude to black women, which can be very uncomfortable for them. There is a significant number of corporate organisations that will say they promote women, however, when you look at the hierarchy you will see very few black or Hispanic women at the senior levels even though they may be well qualified. Often they may be engaged on a consultant basis, however, they are unlikely to be paid well and the conditions seem to be on a take it or leave it basis.

Facing the Challenges

Ryan believes that when men in positions of power begin to understand the challenges, they begin to evaluate their talent, expanding their teams or moving people who are not performing well and replacing them with people, especially women, who are performing well who can bring more value. It's not about trying to supplant and replace men, but about investing the company's finances to help the company grow with the benefit of the best people, which includes women who are not getting the opportunities.

To Young Women

To a young woman entering the workplace, Ryan recommends that she enters with the mindset that her current role is a stepping stone to help her get where she really wants to go. She therefore needs to know who she is and what her value is. If she wants to be a CEO or has plans to own her own company, she needs to think of her current position with this in mind. She is in her current role to work; she needs to see it as working for herself as much as the organisation she is working with without saying it out loud. However, contributing in her current role and gaining experience will make her better for whatever she wants to do in the future. This applies whether it involves being promoted within her current organisation or reaching a plateau within that environment and moving on elsewhere where she can achieve her objectives. This approach is not for the fainthearted or women who want to get a job they work in for the next 30 years until they retire.

Inspirational Women

Over the years, Ryan has been most inspired not by a famous person you hear of on television, but by his mother who had a great work ethic. She taught school for 38 years and still came home and prepared dinner for all five of her children.

Ryan also speaks of Kim, the woman he married who works as a Vice President of Nursing for a hospital chain. Over the years Ryan has watched how she does her job and adds value in a manner that meant that people started recognising her and offering her opportunities and promotions even when she wasn't looking for them.

Ryan explains that while hospitals and medical environments can be very intense and stressful with a lot of pressure and deadlines to meet, Kim is very diplomatic with an uncanny ability to manage a boatload of work. Ryan describes her as the 'Queen of Diplomacy' with patience that he does not have and the ability to diffuse situations. He says she also has great positivity in a very challenging environment.

Awakening to Privilege

J ulian Burton is an Organisational Development
Practitioner with a background in Visual Arts. Working
with his company Delta7 he supports organisations in
bridging the gap between strategy and implementation
using visual dialogue to enable teams to make visual sense
of change by creating stories and making space for people
to grow and thrive together.

Julian enjoys working with women. He finds them to be more aware
of what's going on relationally and easier to work with than many
men. He believes they tend to bring a lot more relational value that
may not be noticed, or may be ignored. Without an awareness that
we are part of a patriarchal culture that we are all socialised into,
the caring value of women at work is often invisible, denied and
unacknowledged.

Julian has recently become more aware of how much things are
done from a very masculine point of view, whether it's designing
toilets to a system of law with everything in between. This means the
value of women is at times ignored or invisible. As men are typically
brought up not to share their feelings while striving and competing,

they are not always aware of this. Julian believes even when you think of Maslow's Hierarchy of Needs, it has individualisation at the top. This, says Julian, makes him feel he has been brought up with a masculine point of view that focuses on striving for independence and being one's best self and competing with others as the pinnacle of adult development, completely ignoring or not recognising the needs of others. This is a product of Enlightenment thinking, which is typically based on male philosophy which again focuses on the individual e.g.' I think therefore I am'. Julian believes that relationships are, however, primary to us. We were in relationships before we could speak. However, we can often feel uncomfortable talking about relationships as they are a taboo subject in a culture which increasingly focuses on the individual, driven by hidden agendas and vested interests. Women, however, typically tend to have more of a relational approach based around relationships and feelings, but this is very much undervalued. Thinking back to school, Julian reflects on how the boys hit each other and played football, while the girls tended to sit in the corner talking about each other and the boys. It may be seen as stereotypical, however, it reflects his experience and there are many people that have written about this.

Maslow's Hierarchy of Needs

Julian explains that in his experience, because women have a more relational approach to work, they tend to have more thought for the whole and seem to strive less about working egotistically. This means the work environment bene-fits from a more interdependent and collaborative approach with the focus on service and caring for people, rather than competing and striving to be the best. Julian believes more people benefit from such a collaborative approach. Collaboration is important for building trust and developing creativity and innovation. A collaborative approach is more productive than one in which everyone is focused on individual goals. Women also tend to bring additional feminine values such as vulnerability and psychological safe spaces, which are also beneficial.

To further highlight the relational practices that women bring to the work environment, Julian highlights the work of Joyce Fletcher's book, "Disappearing Acts: Gender, Power and Relational Practice at Work". From Fletcher's research on the value of relational working, he highlights her four "relational behaviours" that make project work more successful:

- Preserving – focusing on task: Shouldering responsibility for the whole in order to preserve the life and well-being of projects
- Mutual empowering – focus on other: expanding the definition of outcome to include outcomes embedded in others such as increased knowledge or competence
- Self-achieving – focusing on self: using relational skills to enhance one's abilities to achieve goals
- Focusing – creating team experience: creating background conditions in which group life can flourish and the feeling of team can be experienced

Regardless of the value women bring, in his visualisation work around organisation strategy, Julian has found that men are more inclined to put themselves forward and dominate conversations, at times talking over women, at times being closed to challenge and feedback. Women often seem to struggle to be heard in such environments. When they do have the confidence to speak, they are at times described as being pushy.

Julian's awareness increased when he opened up a little crack in his consciousness largely through conversations with a very good female friend who is a feminist who runs a charity opposed to female genital cutting. Over time, she has pointed out gender inequities to him. While he could never walk in her shoes; his interactions with her have been like walking alongside someone and sharing her experiences, making him aware of the privileges he as a white man was previously blind to. In addition to wanting to help to shift the gender balance, perhaps even more important, Julian is now working to manage his own psychological state and continues to increase his awareness. Even though he does not have a direct experience of being a woman or someone of colour, he is learning to spot things that are wrong so that he can respond appropriately and offer his support.

Julian would like to see a change in the mindset of men who continue to act patriarchally and to see a 50-50 Gender balance across different spheres. Julian believes there is a lot of fragility around discussing issues around gender and diversity as a whole. To enable the necessary changes to take place, he feels we need to be more resilient and robust in our ability to manage our state and develop a positive attitude towards constructive conflict (of opinion) whereby we can use conflict to harvest the fruits of change and innovation rather than suppress challenges around gender equality and diversity as a whole or turn discussions on the subject into fights. This requires holding back judgements and demonstrating a curiosity about others and their actions, leading to the polite querying for explanations when people do or say things that are inappropriate. This would ideally be at the time but if this is not practical at the best opportunity as soon after the event as possible.

Ultimately, in addition to the role for men to take some responsibility for bringing about change to realise the value of women, Julian believes there is a need for all of us to learn to manage our internal states better in order to be better able to respond to each other more productively and kindly in everyday moments at work when the tensions and stress around social injustices, racism, misogyny and biases occur.

Conscious Shifts & Leadership

Keith Howells is the Managing Partner of Project Learning Lab, a consultancy that provides accelerated, immersive and experiential learning programmes. He was previously a Chief Design Engineer at Rolls-Royce having worked with the organisation for over 20 years as a Mechanical Engineer. He has also been a Business Mentor for the Prince's Trust since 2014.

When Keith started working at Rolls-Royce in the late 90s, there weren't many women as a percentage of engineers working in Engineering. As he progressed in the field over the next 20 years and took on various management and leadership positions, Keith saw a gradual increase in the number of women in the field over time. Keith believes this is great. He also believes it is possibly a key reason for the increased number of females over time is because of role modelling. In the early years in his career, there weren't many prominent examples of women in the profession and it probably didn't help younger females who were making educational or career choices to see engineering as an option. He doesn't believe it was actively promoted to females in schools and universities as it is now with professional bodies actively targeting women through various promotions to make it a more attractive route for them. This has created a snowball effect which has led to more visibility and success of women in the career over time, making engineering a more viable career for them. It has, however, taken time to manifest.

Working in more senior leadership positions as he progressed also meant working with people outside of Engineering in other functions such as Programme Management, Finance, Marketing, Human Resources and Purchasing. This meant working with more women. Keith now jointly runs a consultancy firm, Project4 Learning Lab with a business partner who is a woman.

Feelings

Based on his experience of working with women, Keith finds women to be more transparent about their feelings. We all have the propensity to hide our feelings and put fronts up, but women seem to be more transparent and better at showing empathy. Working with women who are empathetic has encouraged Keith to share more of his thinking, and this has led to better outcomes at work. Sometimes men tend to focus on how to get the job done and related outcomes. Women are more inclined to view things holistically in terms of the person and consider the team dynamics with a focus on the we, with discussion of what we're doing; how we're doing it, why we're doing it, and how it feels to be doing it.

Keith believes it is beneficial for people to be able to talk about how they feel whilst working together. If the work is relatively simple, with a direct cause and effect, then not talking about how people feel and just being purely transactional and focused on the task is probably good and quite efficient. However, there is very little work like that; things are typically complicated and complex. In such situations, taking a more broadly balanced view that draws on different perspectives leads to better outcomes for everyone.

To highlight his point, Keith mentions his business partner, who was also a colleague of his when he worked at Rolls Royce. Keith believes she brings a lot of herself into the space when she's leading teams. When a team they are working with has been faced with difficult and challenging times she has shown vulnerability. In the past, this has given Keith and other colleagues permission to do the same and express how they feel. Whilst in the past, she may have perceived this as weakness, Keith has actually seen it as strength. The demonstration of vulnerability within teams they have worked in has helped to develop trust within those teams.

There is a subconscious norm that men don't share their emotions or talk about their feelings. At first it was therefore briefly uncomfortable for Keith to deal with emotions within the work environment. However, once he got past the barrier of this not being something done in professional settings and reminded himself that we are human and therefore interact on a human level, he was fine. He then went on to recognise the role of the emotions in helping to build trust, empathy and rapport.

Diversity of Perspectives and Opinions

Keith also values the increased diversity of perspectives and opinions gained from having women on a team. It means that you have different people looking at the same thing with totally different filters or totally different lenses through which they see things, providing highly valuable, broader thinking and perspectives.

Entitlement

Keith speaks of a social experiment he heard of from Joshua Isaac Smith in which a group of men and women was asked to solve a problem and decide on what they would pay themselves for the task with the value ranging between the sum of nothing and $2.50. There was a noticeable difference between how men and women viewed their performance of the task and how they decided to reward themselves. Not knowing the results from the exercise, both the men and women believed they had performed worse than others in the study. However, while the women paid themselves based on their perception of their performance; the men paid themselves based on their feelings of self-esteem, i.e. not on the task, but how they well they thought of themselves. The conclusion of the study was that women may have a lower sense of entitlement.

Keith also highlights a Hewlett Packard study that shows that men apply for jobs when they only have 60% of the qualifications, while women won't apply unless they have 100% of the qualifications and therefore filter themselves out.

Keith finds it interesting that how the differences in how we perceive ourselves and what is possible, together with how we believe we will be judged, affects us. He has seen this in his own experience in terms of the people who put themselves forward: Men tend to put themselves forward more than women and tend to have less doubts when it comes to self-promotion and self-advancement. It would be easy for a manager to simply respond to the request of the man who puts himself forward at the risk of leaving others out. It takes a conscious choice as a leader to decide to take a broader view and look at everyone before making a decision.

Keith believes this highlights a greater requirement of transparency, sharing and discussion about progression, promotion and pay to level up perceptions. This, he believes, would best be led by people in positions of authority with status and influence.

Not a Zero Sum Game

While some may fear that men lose out if women gain in the workplace, Keith doesn't see things this way; it doesn't make sense to him. If you just look at men as an amorphous mass, they're still competing with each other to win, whatever winning means. Keith understands the maths of a hierarchical structure with limited space at the top, but it's not how he views things. He believes in a meritocracy, while not being so naïve as to ignore the reality that men are more likely to attain opportunities than women due to both hidden and visible barriers that exists in both the world of work and in society such that the playing field is not level. He has, however, never understood the thinking that if one wins the other loses and ponders whether it is perhaps an expression of insecurity i.e. someone saying that there could be someone better than me and if they are better than me, then I'll lose my status and position. As Keith sees things, if the other person i.e. the woman, is better than you, she is more deserving of the position than you. On the other hand, if the man is better, he has nothing to worry about. The question then arises as to what barriers and biases exist that prevent the creation of equality of opportunity and true meritocracy.

Keith recognises that it has taken an active process of targeting females to bring about equal opportunities for them and the change that has taken place to date. He does not, however, support the idea of quotas that damage meritocracy and actually create a lack of equal opportunities because they are not looking for a particular type of person i.e. white men, but want people that are different. This he believes can be damaging. He does, however, believe there is value in target-setting to help flush out the barriers that prevent equal opportunities. Targets do need to be based on realistic numbers to create a challenge to ensure everyone is provided with an equal opportunity, but not so high as to lead to less or even unqualified people being put in positions to make up the numbers.

Pay Equity

Keith does not believe there should be any gender inequity when it comes to pay. If men and women are at different levels within the organisation then there will be differences in pay. However, within job roles, he can't see any justification for pay differences. In many ways, it comes back to Conscious Leadership and the ability to look beyond the obvious and not just rely on people putting themselves forward for pay increases and promotions. Keith feels strongly that true leaders need to be able to look beyond the obvious and not just transact on the basis of who knocks on their door.

Women Who Inspire

For women who inspire, Keith didn't need to go much further than some of the women in his own family. The two that stand out the most are his grandmothers. Keith's paternal grandmother passed away around 10 years ago. However, it was only recently while talking to his dad who had worked in the Steelworks in South Wales, that he learnt that his grandmother had herself been to night school where she had studied welding in the early 1980s when welding was very much a man's job. While studying she had been the only woman in her class which must have made it a big step for her. Although she didn't go on to work in industry, she used the skill for creating garden designs, ornaments and lattice work. Keith finds it incredible that she had the curiosity and drive for self-improvement that made her take such a huge step into what was very much a male domain. This is especially fascinating in the wider context of the discussion around engineering. Keith's paternal grandmother also worked as a cleaner in the local school, prior to which she had worked in the munitions factories during the War. She'd also worked as a maid on a big estate and so she had a very varied career outside of the home.

Keith's maternal grandmother is still alive. She lost her husband (Keith's grandfather) 20 years ago. She also lost her son (Keith's uncle) to cancer a year later and then her mum two years later. Three years later she herself got cancer, but was able to go through the treatment, fight through with a smile and overcome it, never losing perspective through the whole process. Keith reflects on the strength she exhibited in order to be able to carry on and finds it breathtaking that she had the stoicism and mental strength to fight through.

Younger Generations

Thinking of younger women from the context of his daughter, there are three key things that Keith has to say:

Be kind to yourself; be authentic and have the confidence to show yourself, but also know your value. Know what you're doing for others and just be honest and strive to be excellent.

Be kind: understand and notice the effect you have on others. The effect you have on others is not always obvious, but be kind and appreciate the positive things you do for others. Recognise that the way people are is just a combination of their education and experience. We are all at different places at different times. As such, meet people where they are.

Make tomorrow better than today. If you see injustice, challenge it, but focus on those things you can control or influence and if they allow you to knock barriers down, then enable others to stand on your shoulders.

Knowing Without Knowing

—————

I an Hale is an Executive Coach with an emotional connection to C-suite Senior leaders globally. In his consulting and coaching, Ian aims to contribute in such a way that the world becomes a place for his grandchildren to grow up in that is full of people who are kind, compassionate and loving.

Including Men

It's easy for women to want to dissociate from men on the basis of past negative experiences. However, Ian believes that if women ostracise all men based on the behaviours they may have encountered with some men, women limit men's ability to support them in changing areas of the environment that need to change.

A Family Background of Great Women

Ian's paternal grandmother was a Russian Jew who emigrated to England with her family. Unfortunately, Ian didn't get to know her properly as she died when he was about five years old. His maternal grandmother is one of his heroes. Born in 1900, she lost one of her brothers and her fiancé in the First World War. After the war, she travelled by train from Liverpool where they lived to France to find out where her fiancé was buried, going on to visit the huts where her brother and fiancé would have stayed during the war. She was a great storyteller and a strong woman with an incredible generosity which Ian learnt from her.

Ian also speaks highly of his older sister, who is three years older than him. Even though he was disappointed that she didn't always have the same opportunities as Ian and his brother were given, he learnt a lot about the world through her, most especially when she became the secretary to the Captain of the QEII and sailed the world. Ian is also married to an incredibly strong woman who has been a great support to him through the years.

Historical Impact

Ian believes that sometimes women may be self-sacrificing and don't always stand up for themselves. He understands this is historical and down to a cultural mismatch about strength and power which still affects women. Ian reflects on a project working with the United Nations and World Health Organisation. They did an exercise with a group of 20 Senior Executives, asking the participants to take a step forward or backwards based of their responses to questions which reflected privilege and opportunities. The eighteen men in the group all stepped forward significantly more than the two women in the group who both ended up stepping backwards. During a break both women confided in Ian that one of the men in the room had asked one of them to get him coffee and another to do some photocopying, even though both women were themselves Board Members.

On a more positive note, based on his observations during the exercise, the Japanese Minister who was present committed to going back to his country and changing the way women were seen in his organisation. Ian found the whole experience mind-blowing. On one hand, he became more aware of the challenges, realising that not everyone sees the world of women in the way that he does. On the other hand, there was the mind-blowing awareness from the experience with the Japanese Minister that if we can get people to understand we can really change things.

Trying to Beat Men at Their Silly Games

Ian doesn't have a daughter. However, he always tells his sons to make sure they respect women as his whole mantra is to communicate with love, respect, kindness and compassion. If Ian did have a daughter, he would tell her not to try to beat men at their silly games because they're playing a game women don't even know the rules of. He thinks some women believe they need to act like men and have the same attributes as men to beat them at their game. However, if women don't engage with the game in the first place, there's nothing to beat them at.

This raises the question: how can women progress if they're not playing the game? Ian explains, if you put your finger in a candle flame and your finger gets burnt, you learn not to put your finger in candle flames so as not to get burnt by the heat from the candle. Sometimes our experiences lead us to think that not only should we avoid the equivalent of candles, but we should also avoid barbecues, radiators and even gas rings, exercising extreme precaution. In the same way if women determine there's a game afoot and they need to compete, they put out a message they are competitive and the response from men may be to compete with them, even if there's nothing for them to compete over.

In response to the argument that men seem to do well by competing, Ian highlights a British TV series, "I'll Get This" which brings a group of celebrities together over dinner to compete against each other through a series of questions to determine who will pay the bill. In one particular episode of the programme, the question of how you measure success was raised as each celebrity was successful in their own way. This episode featured Stacey Solomon, an English singer and television personality. Ian points out that in her responses, she was very compassionate and loving towards the other contestants. "You can't beat that" says Ian. "When a woman brings her utter compassion and ability to be caring and nurturing, together with all the other things that society seems to say you can't bring to the workplace, when a woman brings this, it's unbeatable. There's nothing to compete against, because love just takes over."

Levelling Up and Allowing Women to be True to Themselves

On the challenge of how women can get to senior positions like men who play games and operate in the manner they do, Ian says there is a need to level up. Men who are outside of this as colleagues or spectators, together with wider society have to find the strength and voice to stop it. And Ian pondered, "That includes me." Ian was one of the first people to join the Women's Equality Party when it was set up in the United Kingdom in 2015 and went out to support it when it was launched.

In Ian's mindset, the idea of disadvantaging a woman at any time is jaw dropping. He knows the game that is being played and believes he should nicely restrain his fellow males from doing it. In the past, Ian challenged the members of a Board he was invited to join about their lack of diversity and told them they've got to change things. The same applies specifically in relation to women.

There is a need to change from a system based on self-promotion in which there is documented evidence that women are less likely to engage in, to a merit based approach which focuses on abilities.

Ian speaks of working with a virtual team of a telecoms company. During one of the sessions, two of the women in the team spoke of their need to concentrate more on their empathetic side. He knew the answer, however, Ian challenged why they'd actually closed it down in the first instance. He already had a good idea of what the response would be on the basis of his experience of coaching a Senior Executive at a major Distribution company. She had moved up the organisation over a 25 year period to Board level and was the only women on the Board. Through her journey, she has had to work very hard to be true to her personality and this has at times worked against her. As such Ian understands the game exists. It's similar to his understanding that there is a bias on the basis of skin colour without having a full under-standing of what it's like for people of colour. He's visited places in Africa where he's been the only white person present, but he's never felt ostracised. He does, however remember going into a pub with a black person 41 years ago when everyone stopped talking and turned around to look at him. Ian therefore tries to have some compassion and understanding for people in such circumstances.

Women's Time of the Month

Ian speaks of a female friend and colleague who does work with organisations that reflects on the impact of women's periods on their work. From speaking to her, he has learnt that some women are their strongest and have a surge of energy during their periods, while there are others that may suffer and struggle and need time out, as is the case with his friend.

Ian reflects on a recent conversation he had with a woman he has been friends with for over 20 years who he also works with. During the conversation, she reminded him of a programme they had recently run together. During the programme Ian had asked her to write something on the board. She had been wearing a pair of white trousers on that day and unexpectedly her period had started. As a result she had been petrified of possibly leaving a stain on either the chair she was sitting on or her trousers. Due to this she was actually sitting on her phone. During the conversation, they had explored what such situations can be like for women. Truth be told, as is the case with most men, Ian wouldn't have understood this without this conversation which explained things. For Ian it was embarrassing that he was in his late fifties and he had never considered this before. Society, let alone the workplace, rarely allows for such conversations though.

As a result of this conversation, Ian is now much more cognisant when delivering programmes. He makes it clear from the onset that everyone is free to leave the room at any point in time if they need to use the toilets or deal with something. Previously, if someone had wanted to leave, they would have been asked to wait until the session ended, the point being made was finished or until they had completed a particular exercise. Now he understands it could be something akin to a crisis and he is not going to get in the way of things. One of the great things about Ian's new approach is it he now creates space for women to deal with personal circumstances without confining it to women.

Women's Value – Human Value

Ian believes it's a shame that the question of the value of women in the workplace has to be asked. After all, what's the value of any human being? Ian points out that they are no less valuable than men. They are people that can do great work and there is a need for more of them in senior leadership positions. Ian believe if you ask people about positive leadership role models, Ian has found in the last year that the names that consistently come up are Barack Obama and Jacinda Ardern. Ian believes that key to Jacinda's high approval and success is that quality of vulnerability that she brings. He adds that vulnerability should not be equated to a lack of strength. He also believes women have the tendency to lead, to care, to enquire and not just dive into solutions.

Ian believes women need to learn not to put themselves second; they have as much right to exist in this planet as everyone else. He appeals to women to feel free to teach men what they need to know about them. The more they do this; the quicker women will be able to get to leadership positions. He also believes that it will lead to leadership being based more on compassion and the willingness to understand and listen.

Ian concludes by reflecting on how he can continue to develop and grow in his support and understanding of women. He appeals for women not to see men as the enemy as it is unhelpful to men that want to do more to be supportive of women.

Competency to Create Space

Pedram Parasmand (Ped) works with organisations to design and run people-centred Blended Learning programmes. He uses a multidisciplinary approach to help create cultures for learning, growth and powerful working relationships. Ped previously worked in an All Girls Church of England School and subsequently for Teach First.

There's always been something about giving and supporting others in Ped's work. He previously saw each stage of his career as distinct and different from each other, but he now sees there is a narrative that is like a thread that goes through it, which involves working with individuals for the collective good. A significant amount of that work is and has been in female dominated or orientated environments. Even with the work he does now, he often finds himself to be the only male consultant in the team that is working with an organisation. This leads to the question as to what it's like for Ped as a man working in female dominated environments: a reversal from what is so often the case. For Ped this is okay; he hasn't had much exposure working in male dominated environments to be able make a comparison. However, he doesn't conform to a masculine stereotype of bravado and egotism. Working with females has not been without challenge and he has developed and learnt a lot over time and he is still learning.

From Education to The World of Work

A key reason Ped became a teacher was in the bid to help increase educational equality in terms of outcomes and opportunities after school for students from all backgrounds. With girls, statistics show that they do better than boys academically. There is, however, the legacy of a patriarchal structure woven through society, sometimes more obvious than other disparities that exist within our systems. This can be limiting for females.

Ped believes everybody in the world has perspectives to give and when we exclude females, at least half of the world and their perspectives are lost i.e. all their insights, wisdom and lived experiences. It makes looking at any particular challenge or seeking solutions just partially sighted.

The Value Women Bring

Ped has a deep value of fairness and equality. He has been lucky to have great role models in his life, both male and female. Not valuing the females' side of the equation doesn't seem fair to him. He feels the visceral sense of unfairness, whether it relates to gender or other areas of inequity.

When you think of masculine and feminine characteristics, it's not to say women are all one way and men another However, as Ped sees with his female colleagues, women do tend to be much more considerate and caring in nature than the archetypal male. Ped believes the world needs such traits and since more women have those traits, we need women. He recently had access to some research around ethical investments and discovered that funds managed by women or a mix of women and men outperformed other types of investment funds which are more male dominated. The argument is that when women are involved they tend to take a much more considered approach in making choices, there is more resilience, and more opinions are sought and heard. This enables better decision making; it highlights the value that women are bringing to what we traditionally see as a male dominated world.

Dominant Female Hostility

Conversely, Ped speaks of the experience of seeing masculine characteristics in some women he's worked with. Speaking from the perspective of Relational Systems Intelligence, he explains that in organisational relationships, there are certain roles that need to be filled for a system to work effectively. It's possible that in the absence of men who are more prone to display more masculine bravado and ego that some women and at times girls in a school environment will inhabit those roles because they would otherwise be vacant. This can be done skilfully or unskilfully. For instance, you may need more drive and determination to bring people along. You can achieve this by being persuasive or you can try to do this by badgering or bullying people to get things done.

Ped recalls a Director in a large organisation his team worked with who was really aggressive towards him, creating the sense that she didn't like him. He would present an idea which she would immediately shoot down. One of his female colleagues in the team would say the same thing and she would say it was a great idea. Perhaps she found him triggering in some way, but it was dumbfounding for Ped. She didn't take his contributions seriously and dismissed him, saying they were bad ideas. At a stage she offered to give him feedback and suggested that he had some weird mental problems. His female colleagues explained to him that this is what is often felt like for women in meetings with male dominance. Ped found this very insightful, and it has helped him to see the world more through a different lens than he would normally do. It's also helped him to better empathise with his female colleagues in certain situations. He's now becoming more aware of things he believes he probably perpetuated when he was a lesser form of himself.

Being Open & Supportive

While working at Teach First, Ped was an extroverted line manager with responsibility for a team. There was a particular lady in his team who was very introverted. At that time, Ped tended to approach the situation with her from a very masculine perspective. Not understanding introversion, he took the attitude that it was a personal development issue and she just needed to work on her confidence and presentation. They would be in meetings with other people and afterwards she would confide in him and say she had wanted to say something and would go on to explain what she would have liked to say. Coming from his own frame of reference, he would try to help by simply responding, "Why didn't you?" without trying to understand her and more effectively support her. This exemplifies a time when he was a lesser form of himself.

Giving Space

Perhaps the most profound anecdote of his experiences that Ped presented relates to working with a female colleague to deliver a programme. They had worked together on a number of projects in the past and were to co-lead a programme they had jointly designed. Preparing for the first day of the programme, they had a due diligence discussion about the outcomes they were looking for, both for the participants and themselves and how they could best support each other. His colleague spoke of the need to feel legitimate in the space so that she could feel totally comfortable and give her best. He queried, "What does that mean and what's the request of me?" She explained that she wanted to rebalance the space in the room by him giving her more space to begin with.

Ped's natural style was to listen to what his co facilitator had to say and then add his own thoughts, creating the idea of a conversation between the two parties. For him this was an expression of trust in a working relationship. At times, it would feel to him as if he and his co-presenter were finishing off each other's sentences and creating a sense of deep harmony. However he agreed to her request even though he hadn't fully understood it and so largely continued in his normal style, just saying a bit less. At lunchtime, when they checked in with each other to see how things were going from each other's perspective, it came to light that she wasn't thrilled. Even though he may not have been saying as much as usual, when she spoke he was adopting an approach of having the last word. When she covered a subject, he would add, "Before we move on" or "To summarise". He later realised that it was akin to an implicit assertion of dominance that he wasn't even aware of. While in his mind he was being relational, for her it was as if what she said was not enough. Fundamentally, there was also the question as to how other people in the room experienced the dynamics between them.

Although it was tough for Ped, for the rest of the programme he held back from speaking as much as usual so that she had a more equal amount of airspace and felt more legitimate in the space as an equal partner. At the end of the programme, it was fascinating to discover the difference in the feedback from what they had received in previous years of the programme. Evidence from the comments showed that people saw his colleague as a leader in her own right rather than the more junior of the pair of them as they had done previously.

Reflecting on this incident, Ped realises that there's a lot of work that's done requiring people such as women to step up, push hard and generally do more. People rarely talk about the need for the more dominant person, i.e. the man, to do work around how to show up and create space for other people. Although some people would see this as making yourself smaller, Ped believes it's more about just recognising the need to create space for others. Men have an automatic authority in most spaces just by virtue of being men. They need to rewire their brains to understand this.

Just by summarising what his female colleague said, it gave Ped more legitimacy in that space. It's a reflection of the patriarchal heritage which is endemic, but something we don't necessarily see. Ped believes there has to be a super intentional, super conscious effort to try to undo this. It's still a conscious effort for him to step back when working with female colleagues. From the perspective of the ladder of competence, he doesn't believe he's quite at the unconscious competence level where he's doing it completely automatically all the time but he is actively aware of trying to control when he speaks.

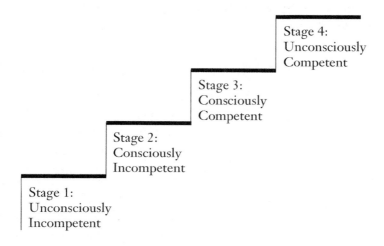

Stage 4:
Unconsciously
Competent

Stage 3:
Consciously
Competent

Stage 2:
Consciously
Incompetent

Stage 1:
Unconsciously
Incompetent

Necessary Changes

Ped reinforces the need for men to be more aware of the size of the space they automatically take up and give more space for others.

COVID-19 is helping to humanise people and create a greater recognition that people have home lives, families, children and all the other things which Ped thinks have predominantly been women's responsibilities in most households even when women work. Within Ped's network there has been a bit more sharing of responsibilities during the Covid period. He has, however, come across reports that indicate women's participation in the workforce has taken a hit as they are having to revert to more traditional gender roles due to caring responsibilities. Ped believes there seems to be some increased awareness within the world of work that people are humans with lives outside of work. People need to be allowed more flexibility to fulfil them, whatever that looks like and with the right mix of whatever they need in their lives.

Having recently got married, Ped is even more aware of these challenges, together with the challenges that come with women taking time off work and pay disparities. When women take time off for maternity leave, there is a loss of income to the woman. This is even more enhanced for freelance workers who are only entitled to statutory maternity pay in the United Kingdom. There is also the challenge of available opportunities when they return to work. Ped doesn't have all the answers to this challenge; however, he does believe things need to be made more equitable so that it's just as easy for men to take on the caring responsibilities for children and it doesn't always fall to the woman.

Ped also believes there is value in more pay transparency within organisations. He doesn't believe it needs to involve highlighting individual salaries, but it would be useful to provide information on average salaries of groups of men vs women. This would allow for more objective arguments and analysis which are less emotive when it comes to pay.

Projecting on Allies

S age Toda-Nation is a Fashion Designer of
Japanese-British Heritage who graduated from
Kingston University with a degree in Fashion Design
from Kingston University, London.

Projections of Male Negativity

Sage opens up by expressing his concern about women who assume
all men think negatively about women. He appreciates that there are
probably men like that, but he doesn't really know any such man. He's
hardly met a man that feels that women should be treated less in the
workplace or anywhere else. He does recall a fellow male student
while he was at university saying bad things about his mum. Sage felt
so uncomfortable with the comments that he couldn't even be friends
with the person in question. He thought the person in question may
have got this from his dad. Sage also believes it's possible that some
men of older generations may view women differently from younger
generations, but he doesn't have many men of older generations
around him and hasn't personally experienced such negativity beyond

that expressed by the student he mentions. Sage is, however, aware that there are times when older men crack jokes about women in a light hearted manner which may not be appropriate; especially when it involves stereotyping women in the workplace.

Sage has had females project their frustrations onto him on the basis of their experiences with boyfriends or other men. It really shocks him that anyone would hold those emotions and resentments towards innocent men that could ultimately be their allies. He found this very concerning as, until then, there had always been mutual respect between him and women. Even with his female friends, Sage believes there is a time and place for jokes.

Women at Work

Sage currently works with a small fashion brand and of a team of 14 people, he is one of the only two men. This makes him aware that there can be challenges with a majority of women in a workplace; he recognises the same can apply if there are too many men and believes its good to have a balance of men and women.

Now in his early twenties, Sage has had four jobs in his life and all of his bosses to date have been female and so he's never actually had a male boss to make a direct comparison of the differences in management approach.

Sage speaks of his first manager when he worked for three years in retail alongside five other men with a female manager in her late twenties. While recognising that she is not representative of all female managers, Sage's impression is that it's easier to speak and have an open conversation with a female manager. There was a nice dynamic in the team that he loved. Sage speaks of the competitive nature (and at times inferiority complex) which is naturally ingrained in men.

Sometimes this can be good, but on other occasions it impedes the job. He recognises that there are men that don't like the idea of a female boss, however, he and the other men in his team all had close relationships with their mums who are all strong women. This meant they were comfortable with women in power and weren't afraid of being given instructions by a woman. It wasn't foreign to them and it therefore wasn't a problem for them. Having her as a manager also took away unnecessary competition as she always seemed fair. Things didn't run as smoothly when the male Assistant Manager who at times deputised for her was in charge. Sage reiterates that his first manager is not necessarily representative of all women, and neither is the assistant manager representative of all men though.

Male-Female Dynamics

Sage believes there is a beautiful dynamic when a woman and a man work together, both bringing different things to the table. He finds women to be more accepting of you and what you have to offer without trying to compete with you. It can, however, be problematic when women try to compete and be the same as men as the two are as important as each other, but different.

Sage doesn't think it works when women try to behave like men, but believes at times women have grown up feeling less entitled than men and less powerful, not just in the workplace, but in wider society. As such, they may come to believe they need to be like men to be seen as powerful and to gain power, but it is unnecessary. Women's power actually comes from the other things they bring to the table that men don't have to offer.

Sage's first manager was very feminine, apt at putting any of the men in their place whilst appearing comfortable and proud of who she was as a woman. Besides being feminine and nurturing in nature, women tend to be more observant and aware of things going on that men are oblivious to. Women are at times described as being too emotional, however, Sage believes that in general terms, when women know how to manage their emotions and have good communication skills, they can be better at dealing with stress than men and tend to be straight up about telling you how they feel. Such women tend to talk about how they feel and go on to talk about why and what needs to be done when something is wrong. In the example of his first manager, it was very much a matter of what you see is what you get. Sage believes men are better at dealing with emotions on the surface, but may end up exploding as we all experience stress, we all inevitably experience pressure, and we all have bad days.

Entitlement & Progression

Sage notes that there are a lot of inspirational women in the creative industries, however, while there are many women at the lower levels in the creative areas, the number of women reduces as you get to high levels in the workplace to the end that it's mostly men at the top as is the case in a number of industries. Sage does, however, believe it's more acute in fashion. Contemplating why this is the case, he believe it may partly relate to generic things in life such as women having children and taking time off which is more difficult to do in the creative industries. You want to make it and become who you want to become. You can't really afford to take time off; most especially as a lot of the people who work in the creative industry are freelancers, working on a project basis with different companies and building a portfolio, pitching ideas and presenting proposals. If you take time off to have a child, aside from the challenge to your earnings; you could easily be forgotten by the time you return. Sage reinforces this with the saying: 'You're only as good as your last job'.

Sage has also heard from articles, his mum and lecturers, that there are fewer women in higher level jobs because they don't value themselves enough and push for the bigger jobs while men feel more entitled to them and go for them. Sage is not sure that this will change with his own generation as society is yet to change enough to give women the necessary confidence and assurance they need. Women constantly see men in CEO and other high powered jobs. This probably sends a subconscious message that you're not supposed to be in that kind of role if you're a woman. Trying to imagine what it must be like, Sage believes it must be very deflating for women. He believes that society is changing and there is a need for women's attitude to change as there are now some really strong women who have made it to the top and are filling higher powered jobs in the creative industry.

On this subject, Sage once more highlights the belief that women's power comes from embracing who they are, rather than trying to compete with men or view them as the enemy. Men and women are the Yin and Yang of life and there is a need for balance between men and women. Sage believes the most successful women (and the ones he most admires) are women that actually embrace, accept and aim to empower men just as much as they want to embrace women. Sage describes himself as a man who is pro women. He believes women can be really good in senior positions. He is ready for it and supports it. He wouldn't, however, push or promote someone's work solely based on their gender. He always wants to be fair and not go in the other direction of giving women credit just because they are women.

Cultural Contrast

Speaking of work in Japan, Sage says you can't really compare Japan to a Western Society as the system is very different. Men typically hold the higher positions at work, even more so than in places like the UK. At the same time, women are respected more for staying at home and looking after the children. It's still very respected to be a homemaker in Japan. It's almost more respected than being a man and the breadwinner. This may change, but traditionally men earn an income and give the money to their wife who decides what to spend it on.

Valuing Good People

J ames Barrington-Brown is a British serial Entrepreneur
with a demonstrated history of
working in the telecommunications industry.

James left school in the late seventies at the age of
fifteen. It was an era of strikes, including a time when even
teachers were on strike. James ended up leaving school
without taking any exams and went on to become an
electrical apprentice. During his apprenticeship he had an
opportunity to work on contracts with organisations such
as British Airways, Rolls Royce and Barclays. At the age of
20 he set up his own electrical contract business, expanding
into property development and later technology, specially
around telecommunications.

Roles for Good People

James points out that he comes up with a lot of ideas and gets smart
people that can make things happen. He has employed people without

any qualifications alongside people who are highly academic with good qualifications. He believes that qualifications may tick a box, but don't always mean you can do the job. Ultimately, if you're enthusiastic, can turn up on time and produce results, there's a role for you.

James has a higher proportion of women than men working across his organisations. It wasn't something he planned but he just looks for the best person regardless of gender, ethnicity or any other factor. He highlights his Head of Accounts, who used to work for a FTSE 100 company before coming to work with him in a small business as an example. She does a great job on financial modelling for the group of companies and comes up with innovative models which are agreed with the Her Majesties Revenue & Customs (HMRC). Other women in senior roles that work with James include his Head of Operations and Head of Customer Services, who also turned up, were impressive, like their jobs, and have stayed with the group.

The Value of Women

James doesn't really like to generalise, however, he believes that women are often well suited to areas such as customer services. His experience over the years is that women are more empathetic. When people explain things to them, they tend to take what is said on board and respond appropriately, showing that they care. Women then tend to go on to deal with the challenge firmly, but fairly, with an understanding of the context. James believes this is key to why they often excel in certain roles. At the same time he acknowledges that this varies and there are men who have more traditional feminine traits and women with masculine traits. Women's accuracy and attention to details mean they also often do well in roles that require an understanding of detail such as accountancy roles. James became very much aware of this when running his property business.

When it comes to leadership roles, James's organisations have a fairly flat organisational structure, and he tries to let people take the lead in their own areas so even though he's the Managing Director, sometimes staff will ask him to do things. He doesn't mind whether it's a man or a woman so long as it's a respectful and reasonable request. James has no problem at all with women in leadership roles.

The Treatment of Women

James says that from watching the media, it's blatantly obvious that an awful lot of women aren't treated very well. This has been highlighted by cases such as the Harvey Weinstein and Jeffrey Epstein cases which are highlighted through the #MeToo movement. James says you feel a bit ashamed to be a man, sharing the same gender with such people or even shame being members of the the same human race as them.

James is aware that there are challenges across the world with plenty of countries such as some Arab countries that are far behind and more in line with where we were a century ago. They don't seem to educate women and continue to see them as second-class citizens. Ultimately, it shouldn't matter what gender a person is. Women have brains and should be given the chance to use them. They can do well in fair environments. The poor treatment of women feels alien to James as he believes people are people and everyone should be treated with respect whether it's someone begging on the streets or the CEO of a global organisation.

On Feminism and Navigating

James doesn't believe staunch feminism always helps the cause though, sometimes it gives the impression that feminist don't want equality, but want to erase men. He believes that their approach at times goes too far and ends up creating divisions. James recognises that there are prejudices and that the work environment has been the domain of men for a very long time, but believes in a more balanced approach such as that taken by Sheryl Sandberg, the Chief Operating Officer of Facebook who speaks of the need for women to lean in more. James believes if you listen to her TED Talk, you'll notice that she's taken a constructive approach of sitting at the table and leaning in with a focus on raising the bar for women.

For women trying to overcome challenges and find equality for themselves and other people in the workplace, James believes it is best to have a goal to aim for, ignoring all other factors, believing themselves equal to everyone else. Women ultimately need to ignore the obstacles or they become a reason not to do things.

If he was advising his daughter on navigating the work environment he would suggest that she treats everyone with equal respect. He'd recommend that she works hard and asks for more than she thinks she's worth. He would advise her not to feel downhearted, but if she hears no, she should try harder and keep asking. She should never be afraid to ask for help or be afraid to negotiate. She should always do what she says she's going to do and take credit when she does good things

In James's observations, women are not always good at taking credit when they do something good, even if they do it alone. Men on the other hand tend to step forward, take credit and request a bonus; women seldom do. It's because women tend not to ask that James has a policy within his organisations that salary increases are across the board and not based on requests.

Thinking of his eleven year old daughter who is quite entrepreneurial and has already got a YouTube Channel set up as she's developing business ideas, James is quite proud that she doesn't see being female as a barrier, but goes out to do what she wants to achieve. James believes this reflects what he has tried to instil in her. She's been taught to ask for things she wants and even negotiate to get them. At the same time, she is very kind and giving and sounds like a lovely person.

Reasons to Employ Young Women

Because of the value that James places on people, he has developed a people management model without even realising it. This raises the question of what he would say to managers who don't want to employ young women because they might go on maternity leave or who might be concerned that women may be too emotional. James believes the very reason such managers don't want to employ women is the exact reason why they should do so. Women care, they have responsibility and loyalty. Those things that make them good mothers also make them good employees: you don't want employees who don't care about anything or who don't pay attention to what's going on around them. The women managers don't want to employ are typically the people who are likely to go up to a person who is upset and ask what's wrong and try to help. We do not bring men up this way, but women are more naturally so. This makes it clear to James that the prejudices held against them are the reasons why they are needed. They are also typically loyal. The longest-standing employees are likely to be women because of that loyalty. So they may take time off to have a child but on the whole they are more conscientious and aware of this and don't want to take advantage. You can usually find temporary cover for the absence. The woman involved is likely to help with an appropriate solution, as women are great at solving problems because it's what they tend to do with family and friends. They also have great empathy, which also helps.

The Value of Diversity

James believes that employers that are a little prejudiced need diversity in their organisation as most organisations are now realising. It is not necessarily a good thing to end up with a company where everyone is like-minded. You need that diversity of people with different upbringings because the company's customers will be a mix of people (a lot of James's organisations' customers are women). The women working with him naturally have a better understanding of the needs. James recognises that he doesn't think like a woman or someone who was brought up in Ghana and then came to England. Such people bring a whole difference experience of life to the table. He emphasises that you need that diverse culture in your organisation because you are supplying a diverse culture. As such, he finds it weird that people want to only employ one type of person and then supply the world.

Organisation Culture & Approach

Thinking specifically of women, James re-emphasises the quality of communication skills women bring: empathy, attention to detail and organisation skills. The ardent feminists he knows, however, do more harm than good as they seem to be even more critical of women that don't say exactly what they see. He believes there is greater value in showing the abilities from their achievements than constantly shouting that they are women and don't like what men do. As highlighted by his distaste of Weinstein and Epstein, he sees things very differently when it comes to abuse though.

A lot of James's work ethics and confidence came from his mother, who was a talented seamstress who would make everything from dresses to bedspreads to lampshades. On several occasions he would watch her working until late to finish a job for the next day's collection. Even while working until late, she would make sure the work was done to perfection. She perhaps didn't recognise her true value though, as she didn't ask for much money for her work. Her focus seemed to be more about the self-esteem and confidence that came from having done a good job, which was the real reward for her. She did it because she wanted to help and doing so made her feel more confident in herself.

James recognises that his recommended approach of women showing their value through their achievements works well with organisations like his, where people are treated on the basis of the value of who they are, but not as much so in all environments; such as organisations that pay men more on the basis that they are typically better at asking than women. This is key to why James is teaching his own daughter to ask for more than she feels she's worth. James recollects the experience of the interview for his first job when he was fifteen. At the end of the interview, his potential boss asked why he hadn't asked about the salary. He responded that it didn't really matter as once he had worked with the organisation for a while, he'd ask for what he believed to be his worth and he believed he would be paid accordingly. When James started working with the organisation he put a lot of effort into the job, coming in earlier and not leaving until he finished the job at hand, even if it mean him working until late at night or even staying at work overnight. After some time he spoke to his boss about what he wanted to be paid. His boss pointed out that it was more than what anyone else in the organisation was paid. Ultimately, James's boss ended up accepting James's request as, even though James was an apprentice, he recognised that James was worth it. James believe women can therefore prove and demand to be paid in line with their value.

Recruitment, Selection & More

M ark Cunningham is the Founder of Cunningham Executive Search. He is also a Business Consultant, Trainer, Author, Chartered Accountant and the Chairman of the Institute of Directors, Belgium based in the Brussels Metropolitan Area.

The Mutual Benefits of Part Time Working

In a post on LinkedIn on the 6th December 2016, Mark writes that since he started working in Executive Search, he has often come across a group of very capable and talented people that seem to find it hard to get good jobs. Their depth of experience is, in many cases, actually working against them. They appear to be 'over-qualified'. This group goes by the name of . . . 'MOTHERS'. He explains that, before his three boys go off to school in the morning, his wife has already made 3 breakfasts, 3 packed lunches and helped get them dressed, while he runs around inanely trying to find his car keys and shoes before taking them to school.

Mark's wife also went to work for the equivalent of 4 days a week for 13 of the last 15 years, continuing to add to the 18 years of experience she has already accumulated. Like so many other mothers working on a part time basis, she is very efficient and focused, often over-compensating to prove they can get the job done and sometimes working when they are supposed to be off. They also often have experience that other people lack.

Mark often places women in their 30s and 40s who want to work on a part time basis (3-4 days a week) to ensure they have time to care for their children whilst working. He believes that it can be beneficial to employ women on a part-time basis at a senior level (in addition to other levels within organisations).

As Mark highlights, there can also be a financial advantage to recruiting people on a part-time basis. Dealing with the placement of Senior Executives, Mark says an organisation may have a budget of €100,000 for a role that may be more demanding or need more seniority, than the €100,000 that the budget allows for, for instance, attracting a salary of €125,000. It's then possible for an organisation to hire someone for a four day week on the basis of a €125,000 full time salary. This means the company gets the requisite experience and stays within budget. While it's typically women that want to work on a part time basis, Mark has himself worked a four day week in order to share some of the childcare responsibilities with his wife. It was hardly heard of for men to work on a part time basis when he did it, except perhaps in the Nordic countries.

The Significance of Travel

Mark has found that unlike women, men also like to take on regional roles which involve travel. It may not necessarily involve more 'work' than an office-based role, due to a significant amount of time in the role may actually be spent travelling (driving, trains or flights) rather than actually working. People don't normally do as much work while travelling and in some cases up to two days of a week could actually be spent on the road. There is, however, a perception that regional roles are at a higher level and they therefore tend to look better on a CV than a locally based role. The Covid Pandemic has, however, led to less travel, especially with regional roles, with an increase in the use of technology to facilitate communication from a home base.

Going for Interviews

Mark has found that women are more likely than men to express an initial interest in roles when he approaches candidates. This is regardless of whether or not they are actively looking for a new position. Women are, however, less inclined to ask about the salary than men. They are also a lot more guarded about putting them-selves forward for an interview if they think they might not succeed. Men, on the other hand, will typically bluff their way through if they are unsure. It can be quite frustrating that women discount them-selves, even at an interview stage, if they feel unable to answer a question. He cites an example of a woman who simply said she didn't know when asked a question. After the interview, she spoke to Mark, concerned that she wouldn't get the job because she could not answer the question. Speaking to the employer, they informed Mark that the question she could not answer was one that no one could readily answer and they actually appreciated her honesty. She got the job.

Career Break

Mark believes a lot of women suffer as a result of taking career breaks to have children, when they may take up to a year off at a time. This is especially so in professions with a work style that requires people to work long hours. This reinforces Mark's view of the need to promote more flexible working. He believes if people were honest, they would admit they spend up to 10-20% of their work week doing things other than work. Mark believes working from home during the pandemic provides organisations with organisation-wide staff reviews as it brings greater clarity about what people do with their time.

The Value of Women

Key to the value that women bring to the work environment, Mark believes they are a lot more organised and focused on doing one thing and getting it done while men may tend to work on several projects at the same time.

Women also tend to be more sympathetic to what's going on in people's private lives, i.e. they understand the challenges people face outside the workplace. Men may be better at motivating and bringing teams together; but may forget to check on how people are getting on and as a result may lose them.

Explaining in more detail, Mark speaks of how he has noticed that, in doing reviews, women tend to be a lot more organised, tending to go through all the points and ask a lot of questions. In contrast, men may focus on their own perception of the candidate, rather than letting the candidate do the talking. This may be a reason why there are more men in professions such as sales, especially in areas such as car sales where there is a need to emphasise or even brag about a car's features. Women on the other hand are more inclined to work in areas such as teaching. The format of sales typically requires the need to make a convincing argument, while professions such as teaching requires a lot of patience and empathy. This empathy means that staff turnover may be lower in organisations led by women.

More Barriers

Mark believes women are not always helped by the fact that they are less likely to self-promote and brag about themselves. Men promote themselves by speaking of what they personally do in the work environment, using the word 'I'. From Mark's observations, women are more restrained and a lot more modest. Women are more inclined to credit the team and speak in the 'We'. Mark doesn't believe women should have to brag about themselves, but does believe people have to listen more, especially when they are doing reviews. People need to think more about the metrics they use when doing assessments. There also needs to be a change in how assessments and promotions are undertaken for women who have been on a career break or away to have children. Assessors, quite normally, tend to remember recent events, so if a woman is off on maternity leave just before assessments are done, tend to focus on the time she was away and determine there's not much to assess her on overlooking the earlier months when she was at work. There is therefore a need for HR systems that calibrate everything and make sure things like this don't take place.

Mark also refers to an article, "The Height of Success" from 2006 New York Times}. It talks about the benefits in the boardroom of being taller. At this time, nearly all Fortune 500 CEOs were very tall and so had a physical presence in a room. Women are much shorter and smaller in stature to men. It also cites that, in US presidential elections, the taller candidate usually wins.

Mark believes that the more we have women at senior levels within organisations, the more things are beginning to change. Women will then have the ability to influence the way things work. On the other hand, when it's just men involved in recruitment and promotions, they are likely to pick people that are just like themselves. He believes there is a natural inclination for men to gravitate towards selecting those who are like them. He stresses that they have to be open to a variety of different people when recruiting though. It can be difficult for people to get the balance on this right. Mark again emphasises the importance of the systems and metrics an organisation has in place.

Progression

Mark believes it would make women moving into senior roles easier if they ensure they have a variety of responsibilities in the roles they fill. They should also ensure that their career paths/futures are not dictated by one person. Sometimes there are risks of being held back if you are very capable and your boss needs you to remain at that level to make him look good. Mark also recommends not staying in one job for too long, but trying to work for a variety of people, making sure that the good work you do becomes commonly recognised within the organisation. Like it or not, men are better at self-promoting and it does make a difference.

In addition, women tend to be more risk averse . If they have a good work-life balance they are therefore less inclined to change job. Mark has found that people that move a lot tend to get paid more. This is more common with men and can even happen without changing jobs. They will mention a competitor making them a job offer with a salary increase as leverage for promotion or a pay increase within their own organisations. Men are also more inclined to present their case for why they believe they deserve a promotion or pay rise at a review. A women may be more inclined to wait for the outcome of the review and then argue her case. At this late stage, increases are likely to have already been allocated on the basis of budgets and it may be too late for changes to be made. Women therefore need to be more proactive.

In an ideal scenario, HR functions would have processes in place that mean pay is not based on who makes the best argument. Unfortunately, this is not always the case as there is not always the HR capacity in place for the most appropriate process.

Mark also believes it is wise for women to have a mentor, preferably another woman. It is also useful to be mentored from both above and below your position.

Depressed Entitlement

Joshua Isaac Smith is co-creator of The Imposter Breakthrough and Managing Director of Adapt Faster Ltd. He is a Therapist, Executive Coach and Behavioural Specialist focusing on neuroscience informed approach to mindfulness, leadership and resilience. He currently coaches executives and teams globally.

"Because we commonly misinterpret displays of confidence as a sign of competence, we are fooled into believing that men are better leaders than women."

TOMA CHAMORRO-PREMUZIC

Growing up with Women

Joshua opens with the assertion of his value of women being an African American man. Although he grew up in a patriarchal culture, reflecting back on his life he remembers that most of the people around him since he was an infant were women. These ranged from cousins, to aunts and grandmothers. They were typically outspoken women who were very assertive and all empowered women, whether they were homemakers or worked outside of the home. As a result, Joshua feels unable to hold a bias against women; he wouldn't even know how. Joshua has observed gender bias in the workplace, but he doesn't identify with it. In his therapy practice, Joshua also works with a number of women as there is a greater tendency for women to deal with emotions and challenges they are faced with via therapy.

Trauma – Empowerment

Through his work with trauma, Joshua has discovered that sometimes men and women lose their voice because of the adverse childhood experiences they may have faced growing up which meant that they didn't feel safe to express their ideas or felt a sense of shame, leading them to struggle to express themselves as adults.

Patriarchal Culture

Reflecting on the value that women bring to the workplace, most especially when they are empowered and able to express themselves freely, Joshua highlights that research shows that women are basically more effective leaders. As humans, we live in an ecosystem within which we need each other to exist and survive. For us to live together, there has to be a certain amount of safety and trust; this is a fundamental baseline of humans in a group.

In a strong patriarchal culture, where dominance is the objective (which might be an unfair assumption, but is associated with males) this works against others feeling safe and trusting. Women are much more attuned to these needs to better enable people to feel safe and trusting. They are more able to tune into the feelings of others, but it's much more than that, they are also better able to see the bigger picture. Joshua explains this with an example: A husband looks in the fridge and asks his wife where the marmite is. The wife responds, "It's right next to you, just look to the right in the fridge". The husband is then able to find it. Clarifying the example, Joshua explains that women are better wired to see the bigger picture and that is crucial to leadership. As such, living in an ecosystem, women are natural leaders.

To further illustrate this point, Joshua tells the story of two types of apes that live on different sides of the Congo River in Central Africa: the chimpanzee and the bonobo. The chimpanzees have a type of patriarchal system dominated by the alpha male and are known to be quite violent in nature to the extent of killing orphan chimpanzees. The bonobos on the other hand have more of a matriarchal system, being led by a collection of female elder bonobos. They are very territorial, but they are not competitive.

Imposter Syndrome

The imposter Breakthrough organisation is run by Joshua, a Therapist and clinically trained Psychotherapist, Kate Purmal, a Corporate board Director who used to work in Silicon Valley and Lee Epting, another former Technology expert. Through their work looking at the Imposter Syndrome, they have noticed that there are clear differences between women who suffer from an imposter syndrome and those who don't. Women who suffer from the imposter syndrome have a higher degree of what is called 'rejection sensitivity,' i.e. they take negative feedback personally. (Joshua mentions this also applies to men who suffer from the impostor syndrome.) He goes on to explain their heightened sensitivity to words. Their brains over-prepare them for hearing words that are bad and take bad feedback to mean that they are bad, whereas words that are good tend to be welcomed and heard but questioned through their sense of self-doubt. For example, if someone from Senior Management tells them they need to try harder, they take it to mean they are inadequate. It's like a form of self-annihilation. It is more than feedback to them. It is about their identity and who they are as a person.

The other area is confidence. Women who don't suffer from imposter behaviours have a sense of boundaries. They are able to differentiate what they're willing or unwilling to tolerate and will ask questions. If told that they need to try harder by a Senior Manager, they will ask to talk about it for clarification so they know what they need to do.

The person suffering from imposter syndrome on the other hand is likely to withdraw and become quiet. A more assertive, confident person will ask what do you mean? Can you explain? This will be reflected in women's feelings about themselves and their self-esteem or self-worth.

Depressed Entitlement

Joshua goes on to explain that both sets of women, those with and without imposter behaviours are likely to suffer from what is called 'depressed entitlement', which means deserving less than men over-all or having a sense of lower self-worth than men. This is in con-trast to a category called 'elevated entitlement' which, according to research, is mainly associates with men and is rarely identified with women, On the other hand, if you have 'depressed entitlement', you are likely to have a lower sense of entitlement and will demand less from others. With 'elevated entitlement', you have a very inflated sense of entitlement and will demand more from others. Since most men in studies on entitlement have an elevated sense of being more deserving than others, when they are interviewed for a job, they don't base their pay request on what they've accomplished in the past, or the work they've done; they base their pay request on what they see as their potential to fulfil a role and how they feel about themselves, i.e. their sense of deserving it and worthiness.

Women, on the other hand, whether or not they suffer from the imposter syndrome, will struggle with this. Joshua and his colleagues have found this to be key to why women are paid far less for the same work as men. They have discovered this to be psychological, as men approach pay from a completely different mindset. As covered by their their Impostor Breakthrough programme, this is influenced by culture and requires a shift in women's mindset in a targeted manner.

If a woman suffers from both rejection sensitivity and the imposter syndrome, she could receive eight glowing reports about her performance and two bad ones and focus mainly on the bad. It's not to say that she wouldn't have heard the good reports, but the imposter syndrome means she won't associate with the good. Joshua believes it's almost as if she sees that as being about someone else. This may be difficult for leaders to understand. Call it shame, call it history from family or what have you, but there is something in the person's past that is impacting her. She's probably used to having to work harder than everyone else to get the qualifications. This happens to people from minority backgrounds as well, because there has been so much resistance to acknowledging women and people from minority backgrounds. This is key to why diversity and inclusion is so important.

Entitled and Confident	Depressed Entitlement with Confidence
Entitled with Imposter Syndrome	Depressed Entitlement with Imposter Syndrome

Joshua further explains that research shows that if there are ten requirements for a job, men typically feel they only need to meet four to six of them to feel confident about fulfilling the role, while women typically feel they will need to meet nine to ten. As Chamorro-Premuzic points out, this is a reason why so many incompetent leaders are usually men. He explains that incompetent male leaders tend to focus more on appearing confident than actually being competent, whereas women and people from minority backgrounds tend to focus more on appearing competent. According to his research this is one of the primary psychological reasons why fewer women and people from minorities are promoted to leadership roles within global organisations that 'mistake confidence for competence' and see it as an essential selection requirement for promotion into the C-suite.

Change

This all leads on to the question of what needs to change. Joshua believes it's a difficult task, but there's a need for change in culture to bring gender equality to the workplace and prevent it from affecting future generations. It may seem expensive to invest in bringing about change, but so is the cost of not having a diverse team that can enable innovation Without which a company will probably stagnate.

Young Females

To young females trying to navigate their way in the workplace, Joshua would recommend that they find mentors. They should not try to do everything themselves, but should find a tribe or a group of women and, if possible, some senior men to help guide them. This is the beautiful thing about the idea of leaning in. It helps to create a whole ecosystem of women that are supporting one another along with men who are sensitive to issues of gender equality and the need for more diversity in the workplace. Young women should therefore find both male and female mentors that they trust and feel safe with because that diversity is going to be important in thriving in corporate cultures now and in the future.

Gender Equality in Africa

D
r Olumide Abimbola Ajayi is a specialist in Gender and Development who holds a PhD in Agricultural Economics, Planning and Management from the University of Ibadan, Nigeria. He is currently: Executive Director/CEO of the Africa Leadership Forum (ALF), Director of Business School Netherlands International (BSNI) Nigeria, Member of the Executive Board of Femmes Africa Solidarite, Geneva, Switzerland and Project Director of the CBN-Entrepreneurship Development Centre, South West Nigeria. Prior to this he worked in various executive capacities in the private sector in addition to holding junior research and teaching positions in the University of Ibadan.

Olumide was working as the Deputy Director Africa Leadership Forum when the Senior Programme Officer with responsibility for Gender and Development went on study leave, leaving a void which Olumide decided to fill.

This led him to get involved in the African Union Gender Working Group to design the strategy and programme for Africa on Gender and Development. He also developed a further interest and involvement in wider activities relating to Gender and Development.

Research on Gender

Olumide's work has led his organisation to provide practical training to over 30,000 entrepreneurs from 2008 to 2019 with women making up 55%. In addition, he has been involved in consultancy work to organisations such as the African Union Commission (AUC) and a number of research projects which have enabled him to expand his knowledge and aware-ness in relation to women. This is exemplified through works such as a book on Gender Mainstreaming with Africa which he co-authored in 2008 with Dr Monica Juma, the current Minister of Defence for Kenya. The book highlights strategies to promote gender and dev-elopment in Africa. A further outline of his major research on Gender is included under References.

Women's Value in Traditional African Societies

Olumide explains that in many traditional African societies, women are known to be the custodians of procreation and the bridge that God created to ensure the continuity of the human race. They are therefore the carriers, producers and maintainers of life. In the absence of women in African societies, you know things would not work out, as they are also the organisers in African society who make sure that men and children receive the care they need. Women are also very nurturing which makes them the stabilisers of traditional African society. They also teach younger women how to carry on with life and make sure that they play their role in society. Women are also peacemakers whenever there is trouble in society. When they step in, they are usually able to resolve crisis.

Olumide points out that history shows that there were a number of courageous African women who led in the struggle to emancipate African society from the oppression of colonisation, leading to the freedom and peace that the continent enjoys today. Of specific interest, he mentions that the first Pan-African organisation was the Pan-African Women's Organisation (PAWO), which was formed in 1962. This was before the 1963 establishment of the Organisation of African Unity (OAU) (which was transformed to the African Union in 2002)

Transferability to the Workplace

There is a transferability of women's traditional role in African society to the workplace. Organisations without women are likely to be limited in the progress they make; things won't work as well, leading to disorganisation and lack in the epitome of the beauty that comes from a harmonised environment which is often championed by women.

In the absence of women, there is the risk of missing out key dimensions in what organisations are trying to achieve. To illustrate this point, Olumide uses the case of a project focused on the management of Entrepreneurship Development Centres in the South West of Nigeria in collaboration with the Central Bank of Nigeria.

Olumide's organisation had responsibility for leading the design, the curriculum and the structure for each of the centres. His biggest regret to date is that there were no women in his team, which he believes was fundamental to the omission of integrating a creche into the design of the centre. Olumide believes if there had been a creche, it's likely that more women would have come for training at the centres as they would have been able to put their children in the creche to be nurtured and looked after while they were in the classrooms.

Olumide believes women also bring calmness into the work environment that brings about stability. Where there are problems and acrimony or things aren't working, men often argue over the problems, while women are more inclined to talk things through and calm situations down. He believes that women bring a beautiful way of doing things and a special intelligence to the workplace. They tend to have very high intuition which makes their involvement in decision-making crucial. They are also more inclined to consider the broader implications and options thus creating greater stability within the workplace.

Gender Equality

Olumide believes that gender equality is important as it brings equality and justice to the things that women do and are supposed to do. He mentions that if you look at the composition of gender demographics across the world there is a natural parity between men and women; in most countries you find a range of around 48-51% of men to a range of 49-51% of women. Olumide believes if we neglect the promotion of gender equality we are actually perpetrating an injustice as we are created equal and we should have equal access to resources. He explains that In this regard it becomes very important for us to promote gender equality. There are women that are intelligent and strong who can do everything men can do in the workplace. By neglecting women and running a non-inclusive governance process, we are actually implying that we don't need half of the population. Olumide highlights this point with an African proverb that states, "You cannot use one hand to put luggage on your head as it won't stand." As such, if the world does not promote gender equality both in the workplace and in wider society, it equates to trying to do things with one hand. He points out that this can only cause problems.

The Solemn Declaration Index on Gender Equality In Africa

In Olumide's work, he has created a Performance Monitoring Index based on the Solemn Declaration of Gender Equality in Africa (SDGEA) which was adopted by the African Heads of State in July, 2004 as part of the outcome the African Union first Summit on Gender Summit.

Although the Declarations does not relate directly to the workplace, its 13 articles cover the key areas and issues that Governments need to work on to ensure that gender equality across the continent. This provides the foundation for women to be able to fully participate economically, socially and politically. The 13 Articles cover:

Article One: Health with a focus on HIV/ AIDS Pandemic, and how it affects women.

Article Two: Women, Peace and Security with a focus on the implementation of the UN resolutions 1325

Article Three: Child Rights and the Prevention of the use of children in warfare and the exploitation of children during war.

Article Four: Gender Based Violence and trafficking in women

Article Five: Promotion and adoption of Gender Parity Principle in governance structures at the continental, regional and national level

Article Six: Promotion and protection of human rights of women

Article Seven: Land and Housing Rights of women

Article Eight: Girls' Education and Literacy of women

Article Nine: Signing and ratification of the Protocol to the African Charter on Human and Peoples' Rights on the rights of women (Maputo Protocol)

Article Ten: Establishment of AIDS Watch Africa to track and report annually on HIV/AIDS situation in Africa

Article Eleven: Establishment of African Trust Fund for women

Article Twelve: submission of Annual report by Member States on the Implementation of the SDGEA

Article Thirteen: The submission of a report by the Chairperson of the African Union Commission to the Assembly of Heads of State on the overall implementation of the SDGEA across the continent.

Olumide explains that SDGEA has three unique features:

- It has specifically focused on interventions and thematic areas that can accelerate the promotion of gender equality in Africa.
- It promotes the principle of gender parity which recognises the effective representation of women in governance structures and political participation.
- It has an accountability mechanism that gives stakeholders the opportunity to track the implementation of the declaration.

The Index and Scorecard called *Solemn Declaration Index* (SDI) that Olumide developed helps measure the performance of Member States of the African Union and ensures they account for their actions as it relates to promotion of gender equality across the continent. It also helps to ensure they remain committed to the ideals of the declaration, measuring their progress on a year-to-year basis, and identifies best practices that can be shared with member states. The index and the Scorecard are being executed with the support of "Gender is My Agenda" (GIMAC) Network which is a network of women's movements and civil society organisations that are working on gender mainstreaming within the continent of Africa. Olumide highlights that in 2015, the SDI was adopted by the Assembly of Heads of State and Government of the African Union for the measurement of Gender Equality in Africa

Education

To further increase gender equality in the workplace; Olumide believes we need to ensure that women continue to have access to good education as the lack of education is one of the tools that has been used to disempower women across the African continent. Without good education women have limited opportunities whether you speak of the workplace in terms of a very formal environment or the informal sector in which women play major roles. Education enables women to communicate effectively and promote their businesses. As a result, Olumide believes that education is a key area to focus on to ensure that women gain their rightful position in the workplace.

Leadership & Policy

Olumide also believes the leaders in both the private and public sector need to continually embrace gender equality. This he believes should extend to political, religious and traditional leaders as well as leaders in the formal workplace. Ultimately, everyone should promote gender equality and affirmative action should be taken to compel businesses to engage more women. In Olumide's office, there is a gender policy which is used for areas such as recruitment with the target of making sure that at least 30% of the staff composition is female.

Women's Own Role

Olumide believes women can support gender equality in the work-place, first by being good ambassadors, ensuring that they do things that will demonstrate to Business Owners, Executives, Directors and Chief Executive Officers the value that women bring to the workplace. This naturally creates the space for more women to be included as part of the general workforce, management, on committees, project teams and the Boards of organisations.

Olumide recommends that young women trying to navigate the work environment should demonstrate skilfulness in their roles. It is difficult to defeat competence and expertise with gender discrimination. "If you are good, you are good and people will know that you are good"

Young women should also prepare themselves for the future of work by undergoing sufficient training to prepare themselves for leadership and not shy away from aspiring to do what men can do or seeing certain roles as roles that can only be done by men. Such barriers need to be broken down with women seeing themselves able to do anything that men can do.

Olumide concludes that over time, he has met several African women who have excelled in their chosen careers far above men. He believes that while affirmative action is good in dealing with inequality between men and women, the ability to show quality, high delivery capacity and competency should be the focus of women as they navigate the world of work and politics. He believes that African women can be further assisted in the workplace through the use of mentorship programme straight from school to enable young women to work with various role models from the community level to the continental level. There is also the need for laws to be promulgated to ensure women get the right type of education and vocational training to prepare them for a blissful career and work life.

Muslim Women

A nouar Kassim MBE is a Community Activist and the Director of Milton Keynes Islamic Arts, Heritage and Culture (MKIAC), a culture organisation that was set up in the aftermath of the 9/11 attacks to connect communities and bring people together through high quality creative arts projects and programmes. MKIAC also works to promote a greater understanding of Islamic Heritage and Cultures.

The 9/11 Impact

Anouar explains how many Muslim women were marginalised after the 9/11 attacks because of their dress code and some of the ways in which they behaved based on their different cultures. Most Muslims were shocked by the attacks. Most of them also felt deeply victimised by people carrying out such horrific killings, purportedly in the name of Islam. Anouar further explains the vast majority of British Muslims are law-abiding citizens who want to live normal lives like every other citizen. They want their children to grow up with the best education, to work hard, to pay their taxes, have a good standard of living and contribute to society. That asserts Anouar, is the primary goal of Muslims. Most of them are from migrant communities with the largest community coming to Britain from South East Asia, particularly Pakistan in the 1960s. Besides other arrivals, the Iraq, Somalian and Syrian wars have also led Muslim communities to migrate to Britain.

Education, Empowerment & Opportunities

Unfortunately, Muslim women have not always been prioritised when it comes to education, empowerment and other opportunities within society. Over the years, MKIAC has used creativity as a tool to educate diverse groups of women. Anouar highlights a golden thread project which ran as a series of workshops over a six week period, which included Somalian and Egyptian women amongst others. The project brought together women who are second and third generation immigrations who were able to explore various subjects such as their expectations, children, concerns about losing their cultural identity, job security; and the reconciliation of the values and principles of how they were brought up by their parents with those of the wider community.

From his interactions and work, Anouar has noticed that a lot of second generation Muslim women's primary focus is their family, i.e. being a good mother and looking after their family until their children reach primary or even secondary school age. At this stage, possibly feeling that something is missing, they would do courses to upgrade their education or find work often in the medical field and go out to work, probably on a part time basis.

Islam and Women Working

Anouar doesn't believe there is anything within Islam to prevent women from going out to work. Some women will, however, come from cultures where the values set and expectations are for women to play a more traditional role. These expectations do, however, change with education. With education, most women would wish to work. When they do, they tend to bring an additional richness to working environments they contribute to.

Value at Work

Anouar believes that Muslim women, just like other women, generally tend to bring a caring attitude to the workplace. They are also very organised and reasonable in their thinking. They also tend to have a focus on a common purpose. Although Muslim women may be brought up differently on the basis of their faith which may influence some of their thinking and decision making, Anouar sees them as being of equal value to other women. Unfortunately, the dress code of some Muslim women may lead to a perception of differences that are inaccurate, and to unspoken bias such as views of them being backward, lacking in understanding, uneducated or disempowered. As with other women, while this may apply to a few women, it is not a judgement that should be made of Muslim women in general.

Diversity in Islam

Anouar explains that while Muslims may have a faith as a common principle, they are very diverse. They originate from different countries with different micro values of their own. Their heritage may impact where they are most inclined to or interested in working. Organisations need to understand this diversity in order to effectively engage and realise the value that Muslim women have. There is also the responsibility of individual women and communities to ensure that women are able to integrate into the work environment.

Muslim Women in Leadership

There are Muslim women in Britain in senior positions such as Baroness Sayeeda Warsi who was previously the Conservative Party's Chairperson who is now a member of the House of Lords. There are also a number of other Muslim women in senior and mid-level management positions across the private, public and voluntary sectors. Anouar believes there must be more honest conversations with Muslim women who have achieved great leadership roles. It would be good to have a spotlight on them to inspire more young people, men as well as women. A lot of the time such leadership conversations have a women to women focus. While these are of value, Anouar believes there is a lot of missed opportunity not having mixed gender conversations as well. He believes this would be of value to all men ranging from those who are highly educated and in senior positions themselves to those working in factories. This would help to create an awareness that would reduce some of the barriers that currently exist for women. Anouar's wife is a successful artist in her own right. This is at least in part because of Anouar's understanding of her value and the support she receives from him in pursuing her goals.

Younger Generations

Reflecting beyond the focus on women from second generation immigration to women of the third generation and beyond, Anouar believes conversations are of special value to inspire and empower future generations to understand that they are equal to everyone else.

Home Builders – Nation Builders

Anouar believes that because women are home builders, they also have the attitude to be nation builders if the developmental conversations take place between men and women that enable the breakdown of barriers, the overcoming of challenges and social stigma. He believes it's therefore important for men to support women who want to improve their education and for men to also take an active role at home. He says, the more empowered a woman is, the more the family value is enhanced, in fact, multiplied as, as a woman goes out into the work environment, she becomes an ambassador for her family and the wider community that shares her heritage. It also enriches both her male and female children as they see both their mum and dad as role models in the work environment and become more inspired. Women going out to work also helps to reduce poverty.

Women in a Diversity of Professions

Anouar would like to see women working across a wider range of professions than is the case at present. This would increase the awareness that Muslim women can do anything they want to do both in the Muslim community and the business community. In line with this, MKIAC has five female Ambassadors who include a lady from the East African region of Zanzibar who works in the Health Clinical Sector; a British Asian of Pakistani heritage who works in a senior position of Research and Development at the Open University; an HR Specialist, an artist who used to work as a Social Worker and a lady who runs a restaurant. As Ambassadors they advocate what the organisation does; it also provides them with a platform to share their backgrounds, achievements and experiences as Muslim women which indirectly contributes to the Diversity and Inclusion conversation.

Young Muslim Women

To the young Muslim woman finishing school and trying to navigate her way into the work environment, Anouar would recommend that she finds something that makes her happy. It does not necessarily have to be what her parents wish for her to achieve academically as she can do this at a later stage in her life. Her primary focus should be what will make her happy and fits with her mental health. Previously, Anouar's focus would have been on academic achievements. However, his interactions with College students and young people at the Spoken Word Cafe Night events that he runs have made him aware of the primary importance of their wellbeing and happiness.

Parental Support & Understanding

Anouar recognises that parents' expectations can create huge pressure on young people. He recognises that each household is different, but recommends open dialogue wherever possible. It's important for parents to take the time understand their children and their aspirations, recognising that their children are developing their characters in different societies from the one their parents may ave grown up in. If parents try to mould their children fully on the basis of their own cultural values without recognising the environment their children are growing up in they may create an identity crisis for their children. This can have an impact on their children's mental health and wellbeing, male and female alike.

Where parents are not always be open to hear, young women may need to be confident and brave to speak to them about what they want professionally and from life as a whole. There is wisdom in a young women understanding the culture context of a parents' expectations in talking to them. There is also wisdom in eliciting the support of an aunt, be it a biological aunty or a surrogate aunty who can advocate for them by breaking things down to the parents and enabling a conversation that yields positive results. It's also easier for a parent to accept such a message from a contemporary than from a child. While an uncle can provide such support, going back to the value of women, women are better able to break down barriers emotionally with parents than men.

Feminine & Masculine Traits

C olin Smith, aka The Listener, improves the active listening, thinking and relationship skills of individuals and teams through his own ability to deeply listen to people and hold space, thereby enabling people to open up and share their thoughts, feelings, concerns and ideas.

Be the person you want the world to be.

Masculine & Feminine Traits

Colin believes that both males and females carry masculine and feminine traits. We've been conditioned over time that men adopt masculine traits and suppress their feminine and vice versa. It's not that black and white though. We have scales on either side. You can be very much the alpha male on one side and gentle on the feminine side. You can also have those who exhibit a high number of masculine traits, almost like the alpha female and the gentle male. There are the two alignments. As Colin sees things, men have been frightened to embrace the feminine traits in them. His sense is that the more men do so, the more they will open up the full range of skills that each of us have. In doing so we also start to appreciate the value that others bring. Colin explains this with an example: if he was really focusing on his masculine traits he would not appreciate the female and the feminine. However, he might recognise and value the masculine traits in the female and value those and think a woman is great because she's a bit of a wild girl and can rock with the guys because she goes drinking with them, she cuts deals and can be bantered with. Colin believes that once men become more mature and start to open up the pos-sibilities, they start to realise the masculine way is not the only way and that there are other options. The moment men start to open up to the idea and start to get curious, to get interested and start to think about it, they start to notice feminine traits in themselves and others and they therefore begin to value and appreciate feminine traits in females.

Colin believes that owning his masculine and feminine traits enables him to feel more complete. If he just had masculine traits or feminine traits, he would be half missing. The more he opens up to both his masculine and feminine traits, the more rounded and com-plete he feels.

Doing and Being

One of the areas that Colin has worked on for a while is the idea of doing and being. In many ways, doing is more masculine than feminine in that it is about action; It is about pushing or driving through and getting things done. Being is much more feminine. It's about love, grace, listening and empathy. Colin has realised that whatever he is doing impacts on the person who's the recipient. If he can think and understand more about his being before doing, it will have a more positive and marked impact on those who are recipients of his doing.

He believes that if you really worked on empathy and its meaning in your work then it would become part of how you do things. This would mean that people would more easily see, for example, a coach, a consultant, a salesperson, a producer, etc., as one who has empathy, and it would become apparent in your doing.

He believes you are more likely to be successful if you work in this manner. As such, Colin believes how we understand and embrace both the masculine and feminine in both genders is key.

We are, however, typically conditioned by our parents and care-givers to use more of our masculine or feminine traits based on our gender. Speaking on a personal level, Colin believes he uses more of his feminine traits than a female friend who is more action-orientated than Colin who is more empathetic. In close relationships, we have the opportunity to learn new traits from each other.

Colin's daughter tends to display both feminine and masculine traits. In her work environment she is exposed to the full range of traits and, by understanding and embodying her own full range of traits she is able to successfully navigate and manage the majority of situations. Unfortunately, she can get 'undone' by people who have strong masculine traits. This is probably because her parents embrace and display a full range of both masculine and feminine traits.

Environment

Colin believes we are also influenced by the environments we grow up in: inclusive of the type of schools, communities and areas we live in. The Political Party in power while we're growing up can also have an impact. All these factors can combine to mean that one's masculine factors are chipped away and feminine factors endorsed or vice versa as a person grows and develops. Wisdom comes as we continue to develop and grow older enabling us to be able to recognise and embrace both types of trait in order to become a more rounded human being and business person.

Colin believes that gender impacts on listening skills, as men typically want to offer solutions immediately and fix things; while typical woman wants to listen, be empathic and to understand, without trying to fix. Colin uses the example of a young woman who works as an A&E Nurse. On occasions when she has been faced with a very difficult day she goes home to her partner and speaks about the situation. His earliest response was to try to help by asking her questions to have a better grasp of the situation and to offer a solution, such as to consider resigning from her job if she doesn't like it. The truth is, she really loves her job. What she really wants is for him to simply give her his attention and listen. In doing so she will know she is loved, will feel heard and validated and be able to work things through in her own mind. Their relationship has since grown and developed; she is honest about how she is feeling and what she wants from him, and he provides his best support through his full attention and listening. He still wants to offer solutions, which he gives her when she asks for them.

Colin has seen a version of this while running listening workshops in the work environment. He has found that the men often find it harder not to interrupt the person talking and try to fix things. At times, men may also think they are listening without realising they are only hearing. Sadly, this is a common misconception.

Changing Workplaces

In the past, the man went to work while the women stayed at home and brought the children up. That is not too long ago. Workplaces are therefore typically dominated by masculine traits. Colin believes that as we continue to progress, there's a need to adapt to the awareness that women are not only in the workplace, but are an important part of the world of work. As the world of work shifts (at least in England), a lot of the manual labour that required male physical attributes to get things done are now being done by robots. This leaves humans with a focus on the creative and service side of things in a lot of areas. Colin thinks the female is often better at delivering in many of these areas than males. This gives Colin the sense that it's actually tough for men. He is starting to see the rise of the female and feminine traits.

When Colin thinks of people he admires, one of the first who comes to mind is New Zealand's Prime Minister Jacinda Arden who is operating in what has typically been a masculine role. To all intents and purposes, she doing a very good job and provides a model for good leadership across the world, even though the idea is likely to upset a lot of people, predominately men. Colin believes she's doing and achieving with the use of her masculine traits, but doing it with heart, empathy and compassion i.e. she is marrying heart and head in what she's delivering. A lot of male leaders on the other hand seem to do so entirely from the head as though using the heart would be seen as a weakness.

Being True to Who You Are

Colin also holds the belief that women's success may at times be hindered by the belief that they have to be something that they are not in order to succeed. Most especially they feel that they have to demonstrate masculine rather than feminine traits. Colin believes this is rooted in history. He says if you observe a woman managing a household, you will see her managing the finances and maintaining the home, whilst also looking after the children. There are a lot of traits that she uses in this scenario that are sadly dismissed and discounted because they are not seen as masculine enough. This can lead a female to believe she is not good enough. Colin, however, believes that if she takes these capabilities into the work environment, a woman who dismisses those she uses at home is virtually living a lie, something which must be really stressful for anyone. What Colin believes as more effective is for females to take their feminine traits and add the necessary masculine traits, thus becoming more rounded. In Colin's opinion, women who do this are seen as more genuine, vulnerable, open and honest, trusting and trusted because of it. Colin believes people actually want this style of leadership: a mixture of head (doing) and heart (being).

The traditional lack of appreciation of feminine traits in the workplace which may lead women to feel that they are not 'enough', may also be a reason why women are less inclined to ask for what they want than men. i.e. they don't have the same sense of entitlement.

Waking Up to Women's Value

Colin believes that men need to wake up to the value that both females and feminine traits bring and know that it's okay to embrace both. This may require creating a space for females in organisations to share feminine traits and to coach men in them and vice versa when it comes to masculine traits. We are all constantly learning new skills in other areas such as project management, so why not in this area?

It's a long road to achieve the required change when some men may feel as if they are losing power. However, this is power by position which is an old fashioned form of power. There is also a power by ability. Colin believes what we need to move to is the power of presence which involves valuing and respecting people for who they are and not who they have power over. This focuses on people's humanity: male and female alike. Colin believes we are moving away from purely focusing on numbers and shifting towards organisations becoming human. People are human, whether male or female and deserve to be treated with respect in the workplace as in other environments.

As he did and continues to do with his daughter, Colin believes more in modelling to young females the type of person we want them to be, rather than just telling them. He believes his daughter's development was influenced by how both he and her mother showed up on a regular and consistent basis. If there is one single message that Colin would like to give to any young female on her journey into the World of Work, it would be: "You are enough and never forget this" Colin believes if females can receive and accept this message then things would be transformed.

A Mosaic Analogy.

Explaining that we all bring unique gifts to the world, Colin uses this analogy: a large quilt made out of lots of pieces of coloured cloth of different shapes, size and patterns. Each of us is like one of the pieces of the quilt and we've all got to show up or the mosaic will be incomplete, rather like a jigsaw missing a part. Some pieces of the quilt may be larger, brighter and more colourful than others, however, as Covid has shown, even pieces that have historically seemed invisible (such as people in key worker roles) have now become very visible and important.

On Equality & Equity

Sudeep Nadkarni is the founding member of the Indian operations that grew to become one of the first CMM Level Assessed Centres supporting a global clientele with a 5,000 strong talent pool. Having lived and worked across Europe, Asia and Africa, Sudeep has served as a Global Account Executive on several large blue chip insurance, capital markets and retail banking organisations. Sudeep's experience includes over 25 years working in industry, predominantly start-up firms, first as an entrepreneur, then as an investor in start-up firms and now turning around midsize companies.

Background

Sudeep feels blessed to have been born and come of age when the internet and technology revolution happened. He is also blessed to be a benefactor of globalisation having been born in India with his primary education in the Middle East, secondary education in West

141

Africa, engineering studies in India and graduate studies in the US. He has since moved around the world and is now based in Chicago where he's lived for the past 25 years with his wife of 19 years and two sons.

Sudeep grew up in a family of strong women. His mum, now retired, was a microbiologist who worked and taught in the 1960s-70s in India, a time when women weren't expected to work, even less work in STEM. Sudeep grew up watching his mum work in a field that women were not supposed to work in. There is an equal balance of men and women in Sudeep's family; even with his MBA, he is actually one of the the least educationally qualified member of his family. Many in his family are medical doctors, have a PhD or something in line with this. They are all highly educated, highly motivated contributors to the workplace. From observing the women in his family, Sudeep has seen the frustrations that women face in the workplace. Going into the workplace himself, he has worked for and alongside women. He finds the lack of women representation within the technology sector frustrating. He reflects that fortunately things have got a little bit better now than they were in the 1990s when you would hardly see any women.

The Value of Women

When Sudeep was one of the founding members of a firm in the early 1990s, he knew nothing about Human Resources (HR). He did, however, know the value women brought to the workplace because of his experience with the many educated professional women in his family. At the top of the list is their ability to multitask, which he believes is brilliant. Second is their lateral thinking. Men tend to have a process driven way of thinking; women's thinking is more like a decision tree.

The third thing that comes to Sudeep's mind is women's empathy. Sudeep believes this is a rich skillset that is very positive. The key is having the skills and knowing how to use them effectively, just like with a superpower. It's up to the women to use them effectively, but also important for people to know how to call upon women's skills.

Working with Women

Sudeep believes that he is a better person for having worked with women. It's not to say that he has anything against working with men, but some of the things that he especially enjoys about working with women is that he believes they are less likely to assume things and more likely to give people the benefit of the doubt, having a conversation around what is in question. Women don't hesitate to ask the second question. They do not take things just at face value thus getting to the root of matters quickly. There is a cultural element that also comes to play here, as Sudeep is aware of having grown up in an Indian family and then gone on to work largely in Western cultures.

In Sudeep's experience, Sudeep believes there are no fundamental differences between the skills of Caucasian women and women of colour. He also believes there is a direct correlation between how Caucasian and women of colour view injustice in the workplace, however their reaction to it may be different. Sudeep believes that black communities tend to focus on equality and an equality of opportunity. For women from ethnic communities, there may be more of a focus on equity because of past injustices with experiences.

Add On Game

Sudeep believes that too often when we talk of women in the workplace and gender equality, people think it's a Zero Sum Game when it is not. It's not about someone losing so somebody else can win, but rather an add-on game. He emphasises the need to understand the difference between equality and equity that are often mixed up. He believes there is a need to get the balance between the two right.

Sudeep believes that everyone should be given an equal chance to apply for jobs and get promoted in order to progress their careers so equality is par for the course. Equity is different. It requires a different level of sophistication to ask the question about the nature of the job and what you are to achieve from a goal standpoint. Does it really matter how the work is done as long it is done? Holding people accountable for progress and outcomes rather than activities is paramount because the approach and activities could be different for a woman than a man. From a management standpoint, each of them should be given the opportunities but equity comes in the way you allow leeway inside the company for men and women to do things in different manners because they are built differently so both are important.

This needs to be largely driven by HR because it affects the whole ecosystem of the organisation. You can't have equity in one part of the organisation, but not in another part. It has to be driven by the processes in place across the organisation; by what is taboo and by the symbols of success of the organisation. It's driven by a system where it reflects the life plan of the organism. You can't have one organ of the body saying it has equity, while another organ is basically doing whatever it wants. That would be unhealthy, so consistency is important.

Male Champions & Mentoring

Sudeep mentions that there are companies that have symbols such as men who are champions of women's equality or equity inside the company. He doesn't like these titles as he believes it sends the wrong message. If Person A is a champion for women's diversity, does it mean the rest of the men in the organisation are not doing anything about it? Sudeep believes it should be part of the DNA of the organisation such that nobody has to even think about it.

With the belief that everyone should have the same equal opportunity to apply for a job, Sudeep believes once they get the job, everyone needs to be held to the same standards in terms of outcomes. Management has a role within this to remove the hurdles that may get in the way of people's ability to achieve the goals that people are working towards. If there are to be champions, they should be as an active role, exemplifying what needs to be done and leading, not just as person of the month who has said to have done exceptionally well. Otherwise there is limited impact on the organisation. If the gender agenda is focused around individual champions, there is also the risk to the agenda if such individuals leave the organisation.

Sudeep believes a better model is to have a formal mentoring programme in place where women get to choose a mentor that they want and not for mentors to choose mentees. All successful companies that Sudeep has been involved with succeeded in increasing gender balance by spending a lot of time thinking about such issues.

Sudeep believes that women make good mentors for women. Women mentoring women is something that is happening and will continue to happen as women mentor naturally. He also sees the value in men mentoring women and getting a greater appreciation for the challenges they face in the workplace. Traditional Mentoring programmes are often one-sided with the mentee asking the questions or the mentor asking the questions to provide guidance to the mentee. Sudeep believes that bilateral relationships are best, whereby both are asking questions and learning from each other.

Sudeep also believes there is value in Senior Executive teams working together on hypothetical scenarios that they may be faced with. He sees it as a great Talent Management tool.

In the early days of Sudeep's first startup, when there were around 50 employees, Sudeep knew everything about them, from their first names, last names, their families and children's names, down to pet names! When the organisation grew to over a hundred employees, he found he still knew their names and the names of their spouses, but not their children's names. By the time they reached 500, he could barely remember all employees' names. By the time they got to 1000, he didn't even know everyone coming through the door. There were around 7000 employees when the company was sold. At such a size, mentoring across the organisation, both upwards and laterally across each department, becomes very important.

A Focus on Outcomes

As Sudeep has seen within his own family, one of the barriers that women face in the workplace is the frustration of balancing work and home lives as they were trying to manage the demands of family and home life with work. In his company, Sudeep supported women in creating a balance to these by managing outcomes as opposed to activities. If you are hiring an accomplished person, man or women, you don't need to tell them what to do and how to do it. You need to agree goals with them and hold them responsible for those goals. It then doesn't matter if they're spending ten hours with their children and one hour at work or vice versa as long as they get things done.

Sudeep doesn't assume that everybody else in his team knows or cares about gender balance. Therefore he spends times discussing the issues with teams, reflecting on different scenarios and how to deal with them to ensure they are creating an inclusive environment. Together with his team, they tend to come up with appropriate solutions. Key with this for Sudeep is his ability to manage himself on the issues of work-life balance and gender balance and getting his team to follow suit. There is also a question as to how people feel about the work environment beyond just pay. This is subsequently provided as feedback ,on an annual or bi-annual basis depending on what is appropriate to the environment. This allows for constructive feedback on the culture from both men and women.

An Inclusive Culture

Having determined to have an inclusive culture, Sudeep believes it is important to make it very clear to anyone joining the organisation that it is an organisation that welcomes people from all backgrounds. If there is no ambiguity at this stage, new joiners know what environment they're joining, most especially if it is embedded in every part of the selection process. Whenever Sudeep is interviewing for a position, if there is no diversity in the candidates put forward to him, he holds the recruitment team accountable for this. It doesn't mean hiring someone who is not qualified for the post, but that the team have not searched hard enough. If he is not provided with a diverse selection of candidates, he tells the recruitment to go back and find more diverse candidates. Sudeep believes if you do this for long enough, you know exactly when to push. If you are ambiguous about the requirement for diversity in candidates or any other area of inclusivity and only do things when it's convenient, it's ineffective. Sudeep likens it to hand washing; it's a health and not just a hygiene issue. If people think of it as a hygiene issue, they may see it as optional. However, if they understand it as a health issue, it becomes automatic. Illustrating with the analogy of the Covid Pandemic, Sudeep explains that your mother should have told you, you should wash your hands properly. However, for some people it's only now that they are seeing people, that it becomes a health issue and people are automatically hand washing. It's all about how people view the world.

Sudeep knows this works as in his first start up, only five of the first fifty employees were women. By the time the company went public, around 35-40% of employees were women. In fact the president of the company was a woman and two out of the top five leaders of the company were women. This is within the Technology sector where you typically have lower than 20% women representation.

Key to Sudeep's success in creating a greater gender balance and more generally inclusive workplace is his clarity of purpose, which is shared across the organisation at a practical level. He's comfortable managing outcomes instead of activities. He's also clear on both the importance and differences between equality and equity and knows when to apply each.

Culture & Cultures

D r Sheriff Alabi is a highly accomplished Business Development Specialist, who in addition to a variety of other roles, currently works as Head of Africa Governance, Development & Partnerships at Nation Building Initiative. Born in an agricultural community in Nigeria, he came to England in the 1980s where he has studied extensively, including for a PhD in Tourism Marketing at Bournemouth University.

Background Setting

Sheriff's childhood was spent in the rural farming communities of Akesan and Ijanikin in the Western part of Nigeria. He spent some of this time supporting his paternal granddad who was involved in various vocational activities such as farming, fishing, hunting, distillery, blacksmithing and herbal medicine. His grandfather supplied fish to women in the village who went on to sell the fish in local markets and neighbouring villages. Sheriff's father worked in a wide variety of local industries, ultimately going on to found and run enterprises in petroleum products, retail and building materials distribution.

The women in his family tended to work in the homestead, while also collecting raffia materials from the swamp areas which they used for weaving craft products such as mats and baskets in line with their own vocations. They would go on to sell their crafts in both the local markets and main towns as far as Lagos, the then capital of Nigeria. In addition to her craft business, Sheriff's mother was also involved in retailing kerosene, which is a major source of fuel for lanterns and cooking. The success of his mother's kerosene business meant that she eventually stopped her crafts business. For a long time, Sheriff thought that the first property constructed in his family was financed by his father, only to find in later years that the family home was funded from the proceeds of his mother's kerosene trade. This was quite unusual in rural communities in Western Nigeria in the 1960s as women were not expected to own properties or land. His mother was a very industrious woman, despite her lack of any formal education. (She had never set foot in a school.)

Against this childhood background, after finishing College, Sheriff started working for an International company across various functions including factory floors and Human Resources. He ultimately specialised in Sales and Marketing. He relocated to England to study Management and Marketing in the early 1980s and he has since settled there, visiting Nigeria on a regular basis.

Different Perspectives & Thinking Hats

From Sheriff's experience of both working in, and managing, teams, he has found that men are not always broad-minded and open in their push to get things done, seeing things as almost black and white and no other way. From his time in academia, in government and in the private sector, he finds that women generally look at things differently and bring different perspectives to situations from men. He believes that working with women brings a different energy into conversations, which enables everyone to look at the same situation from a much broader perspective, allowing for the consideration of a wider range of options and possibly better outcomes. He explains that if you think of it from the perspective of Edward De Bono's 'Six Thinking Hats' it gives you better and more positive results than you would otherwise have achieved without the input of women.

In spite of the value that women bring, Sheriff doesn't believe that women are always given the space that enables them to play their role to the greatest level. Sheriff has always believed that women manage situations better than men in the majority of cases. He believes men are more emotional in the way they approach situations. Women, on the other hand, tend to be a little more sensitive to situations and other people's feelings, respecting and valuing their opinions more than men do. In addition, while men tend to react quickly to situations; women are more inclined to sit back and reflect before responding. This motherly hat and approach women take in such situations often brings about better results.

Sheriff believes that this motherly approach is a particularly special management skill and aptitude that naturally comes to women, allowing them to respond on the basis of their reflections, rather than immediate reactions to situations. In modern management thinking, there is the widely held conception that people shouldn't give an immediate response but pause for six to ten seconds before responding or on occasion just keeping quiet. This comes more naturally to women than men who are more inclined to react immediately to situations. A reactionary approach, says Sheriff does not always lead to the best possible outcomes.

Sheriff believes that women's natural aptitude to managing situations means that they are better at guiding and directing. When a situation arises, a man will typically voice what he is thinking of doing, while a woman would think through the options and potential outcomes, positive or negative, and has the ability to determine an approach based on best fit outcomes. This is why Sheriff believes they are better at managing situations and usually get better results. Sheriff believes that most women are more inclined to value everyone's perspective and contributions and therefore carry everyone along. He believes there are, however, women that will take a defensive approach perhaps as a result of previous, less positive interactions in other situations, leading them to be less trusting of people and making them more defensive.

Cultural Impact

Sheriff expresses the opinion that culture also impacts women's interactions within the workplace. In traditional African, Asian and Caribbean cultures there tends to be more of a community based approach to the way in which things are done, so things get done on the basis of the community and how they may affect a neighbour or even a stranger, whereas in Western cultures the focus is more on the individual. Sheriff believes that the feminine traits that are typically demonstrated by women are more valued and freely expressed in organisations where there is a greater sense of community within the wider society. As such, there are also variations within Western society. For example, in the case of England, if you move from cities like London, Manchester, Birmingham or Newcastle to more rural settings within the country there is a greater sense of community and almost everyone knows everyone. This affects the work environment, leading to a better appreciation of women's value.

Sadly some of the Western cultures are overtaking traditions, norms, beliefs, cultures and practices of African societies such that modern African generations are losing some of these values which are actually beneficial to them without fully understanding the values from other cultures that they are adopting. While there is a need for modernisation in African societies, there are risks of alienating and disenfranchising some members of society and leaving them behind in society.

In Western society, teams are typically conceptual. People are provided with codes of conduct, behaviour and expectations for the workplace and taught how they should interact and work together and contribute to a team's potential success, but individuals are still focusing on their own self-interest.

In such environments, women may be seen as passive as they are not asking, demanding or requesting. As a result, in additional to being taught how to be part of a team; women are taught to be more assertive. In the process of trying to be assertive, they may be regarded as aggressive; most especially by men who are not comfortable with women who know their rights and who are prepared to demand what is right and expect it to be given.

This presents a challenge for women, most especially for women from black, Asian and ethnic minority (BAME) communities whose cultural backgrounds have a closer affinity with community focused cultures. This leads to these women's natural feminine skills such as broad thinking, nurturing, guiding and directing not being fully valued in societies and organisations that are more individualistic in nature.

Organisation Culture

As a result, Sheriff believes that there is a need for women to understand the culture of the environment they are in and the key influencers in that environment. Sheriff recommends that they engage with one or two key influencers who can argue their case which necessarily and generally provides them with the right kind of support that they need, possibly as mentors. Sheriff believes we all need someone to guide us as no one knows everything. There is therefore value in having a mentor in the workplace or even from another organisation who can provide external support: it doesn't matter whether the person is male or female. Sheriff believes this is even more important for women from BAME backgrounds who often struggle. Sheriff sees understanding the environment and the expectations within that environment as critical or such women will never be able to fit in regardless of who they have in their corner.

Sheriff also emphasises the importance of social interactions, as the formal work environment is not necessarily the only place where decisions are made. He therefore believes it is important to engage in social activities from time to time. If people are going out for a social drink after work, a woman doesn't have to drink alcohol or stay for a long time, however, the type of conversations that take place in these settings are sometimes greater and more powerful than some conversations that take place in the formal workplace. People are not always as relaxed and open in the workplace as they are out of that space. You learn more about people in such environments and at times learn about what is happening and about opportunities that are coming up before they are formally communicated. Such knowledge means you are able to align and position yourself with the right people and opportunities.

Sheriff believes that, while this may be a challenge for women with children, it's not an insurmountable challenge. They don't have to attend every social event or stay out until late. For instance, if they have advance knowledge of an event taking place, they can make special arrangements for that occasion.

Religion & Culture

As a Muslim, Sheriff doesn't believe things should be fundamentally different for a Muslim man or woman than for anyone else. He does, however, realise that some Muslims may see things differently on the basis of their interpretation of the Quran, Hadith (recording of the traditions and sayings of Prophet Mohammed) and practices. On the basis of Sheriff's understanding, it is not acceptable to shake a woman's hand, However, he has found himself in many situations whereby women, including Muslim women, have stretched out their hands to him and he has shaken hands with them. He does believe that men should not initiate this, however, they should respond to a woman's lead. This would apply in other areas pertinent to faith as well, as different Muslims will have different interpretations and cultural influences. They may also believe it to be appropriate to moderate their behaviour to the environment they are in, as long as it does not directly contravene their religion. Ultimately, Muslim women need to weigh things up and make decisions for themselves in these areas as women from any other religious background. The same principles would apply to women of any religion.

Beyond Policy

For organisations to realise the value of women in the workplace more fully, they need to practise what they preach, to go beyond policy statements and remove any blocks or blinds that exist to see the value of people in order to understand what it really means to value all people and put a support framework in place to be able to better develop, build a diverse strong workforce, meet individual needs and realise the potential of all employees.

Edward De Bono's Thinking Hats
'The Six Thinking Hats' is a role-playing model presented by Edward de Bono. It is a team- based brainstorming and problem solving approach that can be used to explore challenges and their solutions to uncover options and ideas that are likely to be overlooked in a homogenous thinking group.

Different Perspectives
& Lived Experiences

Gamiel Yafai is a Diversity & Inclusion Expert. He started working in the world of Diversity when he was involved in the 2000 amendments to Britain's Race Relations Act. He is co-author of the books, 'Demystifying Diversity' and 'Yemen Proud'. Gamiel is also an Ambassador for the Global poverty charity, The Hunger Project, and a Board member for Milton Keynes' Park Trust and Women Leaders UK.

Background

Gamiel is a dual or perhaps multi-heritage 'Brummie', born in Birmingham, England. His mum was born in Glasgow to a Scottish/Irish mother and a father who was born in Hyderabad, India to Yemeni parents. His father was a farmer born in the north of Yemen who migrated to England in the mid-1950s. Gamiel comes from a working class background, growing up on a multicultural council estate.

Unfortunately, by the age of ten Gamiel started getting into trouble, leading his father to send him, his brother and sister to live in Yemen just before his twelfth birthday. When they left, Gamiel's father told his mother they were leaving for a six week holiday, which ended up being two and a half years. His mother, who they had left in Birmingham with his youngest sister, eventually persuaded his father to bring them back to England.

Yemen and an Awakening to Gender Inequality

A big tea drinker, Gamiel's mum had taught him to make tea from around the age of six. She also taught him how to decorate from the age of eight; Gamiel's skill is illustrated by the wallpapering in his office. Gamiel's mum also taught him how to paint and do carpentry. She was an immense influence on him as a child; giving Gamiel the gift of self-sufficiency and an appetite for trying new things. In many ways, this prepared him for the biggest adventure of his life. i.e. his time in Yemen where he moved between the village which had no gas, water or electricity and the city of Taiz where he sometimes went to school.

Moving to live in Yemen in the early 1970s, Gamiel's experiences and observations of women in Yemen were very different from what he had been used to while living in England. For the most part, he lived in a tiny village in Yemen with his step mother. It was here that his experiences of gender inequality really came to life. Women did everything in the village but were not given the power to express themselves or maximise on their potential. They got up early in the mornings. They would make flour and then bake bread. They would go on to take the cows, sheep and goats from the ground floor of the house to graze on the small pieces of land that were handed down from family to family. This was all done before they came back into the house to bake the bread and make breakfast for when the men woke up. After this, the women would go on to do absolutely everything else that needed to be done in the village.

Gamiel saw huge challenges in the treatment of women by men and the lack of opportunities that existed for them. The boys always went to school but the girls were very rarely educated and were often married off from the age of about fourteen. This deprived them from having the opportunity of having the lives they may have wanted and the opportunity to explore and create anything outside of a life centred around their husband and children.

In the cities, women were all dressed in the full burqa from the age of twelve onwards. Men and women didn't stop to say hello to each other in the streets, so women were hidden. Women were very rarely engaged or involved in anything that went on outside of doing chores and bringing up the family. They made craft goods such as baskets, but for their homes rather than to trade and create a source of income. There was also a tendency for women in the villages to have sewing machines with which they used to make their own clothes so rather than buy clothes they bought materials and made everything they needed at home. In the cities you would find women selling fruit and vegetables in the markets and souks.

When Gamiel was in Yemen in the seventies, there were very few women who went out to work in the cities except for selling produce in the markets and souks. Over the following decades this changed significantly and there are now a lot more women doing different types of work but it is in no way near to proportional representation. There are still very few women in positions of influence and power. Although the dynamic has been broken down a little bit, the power dynamic between men and women still exists. Gamiel highlights the situation in neighbouring Saudi Arabia, where women have only just been allowed to drive in spite of all the technology and money in the country. Gamiel believes that Yemen is even further behind than Saudi Arabia in its thinking and governance. Religion and social status can also play a part. Both the war and COVID-19 have not helped the case of women in Yemen either. Gamiel believes a lot of the problems for women in Yemen come from the lack of role models and leadership together with men not having a desire to change the power dynamics. Gamiel believes that Yemen is losing out financially, socially and economically from the lack of gender representation.

Role Modelling

Back here in England, Gamiel chairs the Yemeni Education Network. It involves around 45 highly skilled and talented male and female Yemeni professionals who go into schools and colleges and speak to Yemeni children and young people here in the UK about their progression and to raise their aspirations. The ambition is for the programme to extend to have Yemeni professionals with the right skills, knowledge and aspirations visit and speak to young people in Yemen as well..

The female professionals include a number of head teachers and professionals in other areas of education, doctors, solicitors and others inclusive of a female palaeontologist who is also a comedian. Ten years ago, this was unheard of. Their presence shows what can be done and that women can succeed in any position. This is as important for Yemeni women in Yemen as those in the UK.

Yemeni women in the UK tend to be influenced by their parents This is leading to increasing change and progression for those that are encouraged to be independently minded and want to explore wider ways of reaching their full potential. About 99.8% of Yemenis are Muslims and this plays a powerful part in attitudes as does how Yemeni culture intersects with British culture.

The Influence of Islam

Depending on interpretation, Islam, as in other religions, can be used to justify why a girl should not be educated and develop a brilliant career. On the other hand, it can be used to demonstrate the duty to ensure that girls maximise their potential and make a difference to the world. Gamiel provides an outline on how Islam actually supports women in education and business:

Islam Commands us to seek knowledge value education and con-tribute positively to society regardless of gender.

There are so many women in the scholarly history of Islam. Dr Akram Nadwi compiled the biography of more than eight thousand women scholars in forty volumes. Muslims should take these great women scholars as role models.

The earliest role models in Islam are two of Prophet Muh-ammad's wives.

Prophet Muhammad's first wife Khadeejah was an educated and respected businesswoman. When she died, he married Aaisha, who became one of the greatest scholars of her time. Other scholars both men and women used to go to her for knowledge. One Scholar said: I heard the speech of the first four caliphs, but I never heard a better speech than the one coming out of Aisha's mouth.

Amrah Bint Abdur-Rahman a student of Aaisha became a legal scholar in Medina. Many women, in as early as the second generation of Islam (just after the prophet's death) became scholars.

Over 1400 years ago people used to dislike it when a daughter was born to them and some used to bury their daughters alive. Prophet Muhammad addressed this problem with education at the heart of his instruction. He said: "Whoever has a daughter, and educates her and takes care of her, will go to paradise".

One day a group of women came to Prophet Muhammad and told him that the men were getting ahead of them in terms of education and knowledge. On hearing this, Prophet Muhammad set extra days for the women to go and learn. This encouraged women to seek knowledge and education in the generations that followed his death. The first university in the world was founded in the ninth century in North Africa by a Muslim woman. Fatimah Al-Fihri was highly educated and founded the university that issued Degrees at different levels.

Arwa bint Ahmed became the first Muslim woman ruler of Yemen. She became queen of Yemen not through marriage to a king, but a ruling queen ruling Yemen by herself. Many historians commented on her great ability and wisdom as a ruling queen. Queen Arwa ruled Yemen for over half a century.

Islam encourages women to educate themselves and become businesswomen: doctors, scholars, philosophers, whatever they want to be. However, through cultural constrains, women in the rural parts of the developing world, have been deprived of this God-given right as advocated by prophet Muhammad. However, even through those cultural constrains, some women managed to become businesswomen Including Hunood Abdul Rahman the grandmother of Gamiel Yafai who lived in a village with male chauvinists, became a businesswoman. On her donkey, she went around the villages selling items of food and household commodities.

162

Male-Female Synergy at Work

Gamiel believes that when women do go out into the world of work, they add additional value by bringing different perspectives and lived experiences. Due to the different challenges that women experience during their lives they tend to be more resilient than men. As girls are seen differently from boys they tend to face difference challenges as they develop and grow. They are faced with more inequality and become more resilient in dealing with them.

When it comes to leadership, Gamiel believes it's not so much about women or men leaders, but about the synergy that's created when you bring the different perspectives together; it's like magic when they come together to explore challenges. When you have to think things through, when you have to design, people talk about diversity of innovation, creativity.

Gamiel believes women's experiences in life don't just make them more resilient. They also bring about a level of knowledge and understanding that provides them with the capabilities to overcome challenges and find solutions to different issues on a daily basis. When you combine this with a male perspective you get magic and brilliant things start to happen. That says Gamiel, is the power of diversity, especially when gender diversity is combined with ethnicity, disability and other areas of diversity.

Bringing About Change

Gamiel points out that as women represent more than 50% of the population, that diversity is huge. He believes there is therefore a need to create the culture within organisations via the systems, processes, procedures and policies to enable that value to be fulfilled.

We know from the Gender Pay Gap that there are huge differences in financial recognition. We need to speed up the change which involves getting men involved in the process. Men need to become allies, advocates and sponsors. When men start to talk about the talent that women bring, it helps to increase the width of exposure, visibility and voice for women within organisations, so men have a huge, huge role to play. Men do need to be invited in though. There are networks that don't invite men in. They therefore miss some of the knowledge and experience that may help progression. Men also need to help in changing the system that has been developed for men. There needs to be a lot more conversation and inclusion of men in the journey.

Gamiel explains that part of Diversity and Inclusion is communication and marketing as many believe, but the real work that needs to done is around a culture shift i.e. changes of system that are out of date, amending processes, policies and procedures to lead to real change to organisations. There is therefore a need to get men onside. It's not to say that a lot of men are not already there, it's just that they are not invited to the party. We need to talk to them more about the challenges, those micro inequalities and micro-aggressions.

Women's Own Blockages

Speaking from a developmental perspective, Gamiel believes that sometimes the biggest barrier to the changes that need to take place is actually women themselves. From the programmes to support women in their development that Gamiel facilitates within the British Civil Service, women are not always confident and don't always see themselves as capable of doing things compared to men. If you present a man and a woman with the job description for a role with ten responsibilities, the man would typically say he's fulfilled three of the responsibilities, he's done a bit of five of them and he's sure he can fulfil the role. Gamiel's experience from working with hundreds of women is that a woman is more inclined to say she has fulfilled three of the responsibilities in the past, but not the rest and automatically deselect herself. Men will blag their way through, women will deselect themselves. As soon a woman sees something they haven't got direct experience of they will create a blockage for themselves and move on to the next thing.

Other self-limiting beliefs such as imposter syndrome also serve as blockages to women. It may be because of a chip they have on their shoulder or what other people have told them in the past, but they need to find ways to overcome these issues and come to the belief that they are truly worthy.

There is also a need for women to be supported to develop more of a growth mindset and begin to think more positively about themselves. Gamiel believes that this is where the value of role models, mentors and advocates come to play in helping them to build confidence in themselves. He believes mentoring for women should include male mentors and even reverse or mutual mentoring.

Men Supporting Women

For men that say they want to support women, Gamiel believes from his own experience that if you genuinely want to do something, you will find a way of doing it. You need to be intentional and proactive. If you take one approach and fail, you need to find a different way of doing somethings.

Find what you're passionate about or think about your daughter and what you want for her and what you would like her to achieve.

What would you do to make it happen? What you would do for your daughter (if you have one) is what you can do to support women in the work environment. If men think of it that way, they are unlikely to give up; it's incredible what people would do for someone in their network compared to anyone else.

Supporting Young Women

To support a young woman in school preparing to navigate the world of work, Gamiel would start by asking her what she wants from life. Very few people can actually answer the question and so the question may then be, what do they want and how can they be supported to achieve it. More important than a career is for young women to be able to find themselves and have the support to do so whatever it is they want to do. Gamiel believes this is about being inquisitive and finding out what a woman is passionate about, hopefully spending enough time with them in their earlier years to already have a fairly good awareness of who they are and what they want.

Gamiel has discovered/observed that a number of male advocates for Gender Equality within the workplace tend to spend more time with their sons as home than with their daughters. They suddenly come to the realisation that they are not doing at home what they are advocating for at work. Loving that daughter is important, however, there is also a need to help that daughter find herself and what she wants to do. It is key for men to dig deep and find things that are of joint interest between them and their daughters. Sometimes it's just about talking to a daughter and asking her what she wants. Talking is the first and often most important step, but listening and hearing are vital for progress.

166

Navigating Environments

J ohn Sulola is a professional with a very rich career
and variety of experiences. He started his career with
service in the British Army, moving on to positions in
Business Development, Financial Public Relations,
Consulting and Education in Life Sciences, Clinical
Research and Education.

The Army

Working in the Army for five years from the late 80s, John recalls
there being female officers in his regiment who had an influence and
led to some changes in the atmosphere, the management of people
and situations. He remembers a specific female Major who was very
bright, amicable and capable, who ended up moving to a very senior
level within the army. John was never managed by a female officer,
however, he had a few female colleagues. The army was, however, as
it remains, very male dominated.

Looking back, John recollects that the female officers had a different way of managing soldiers than the men. In many ways, the

male officers gained respect by demonstrating their toughness and strength. John doesn't believe there was any way that female officers could do that. Female officers gained respect of soldiers through the language and management techniques that they used, which were more intelligence-based such as working out the strengths and weaknesses of soldiers and managing them according. Female officers also tended to take more time to understand soldiers and their families on a more personal basis. Ultimately, female officers looked at things from a more wholistic perspective. John believes there's therefore nothing to stop women from joining the army and adding value as long as they don't make the mistake of trying to lead like men.

The Pharmaceutical Industry

John's first boss when he moved on to the Pharmaceutical industry was a woman who John recalls in a very positive light. Although he has had female managers who weren't very good, most especially those who tried to manage like men, he has found most to be very good, focusing strongly on his potential and capabilities. The best female boss he has ever had was a Managing Director he reported to at a time when he was at the top of his game, who he sees as excellent and engendering a lot of trust and respect. John still remains in touch with her.

John recollects when his first daughter was born. He was scheduled to travel from London to Philadelphia on the day of his daughter's christening. His boss told him to take a later flight at cost to the organisation on the basis that it was really important for him to be at the christening for his first child. In many ways it was a small thing, however, she constantly managed like this and it was things like this that made her stand out. She was also very knowledgeable and capable of navigating to get things done. It's not impossible that a man would behave likewise, however, John believes it comes more naturally with women and they are therefore typically more consistent with being supportive.

Education & the Highlight of Women's Unique Value

In his general experience of working with women, John has found that they give a different perspective and are more mindful of people's feelings, most especially with decision making. John saw even more of this in education, which is dominated more by women. Men on the other are more task-orientated. At first it felt uncomfortable talking a lot about how you feel specifically, how you feel at the moment, and how you may feel tomorrow in the face of major situations such as redundancies. John believes it is good to have consideration for both the emotional and business side of things in such situations. It gives the impression that somebody actually cares about the impact decisions are having on people's emotional welfare and makes it a more palatable pill to swallow because you know they understand the human aspect. The ideal is to have a combination of emotional intelligence and practicality within leadership. John believes women actually do themselves a disservice when they manage in a very hard and aggressive manner.

Culture, Perceptions & Acceptance

Throughout his career, John has come across a number of brilliant and capable women of colour of different ages from places such as

Nigeria where he himself originates from. John believes in its natural form, the Nigerian accent may sound aggressive and harsh to people with more gentle accents, most especially when combined with very expressive mannerisms which are often used in communications. John has at times observed students, males as well as females, who are brilliant, with the potential to work in professions such as Medicine or Law, who may be perceived negatively because of their tone. John emphasises the importance to maintain their cultural norms, whilst also being adaptable. The perception of aggression is not based on reality, but it is an important element. The work environment can be especially tough for black women (and men). John points out that people are often judging you and questioning how you got the job. There can be a number of little barriers and obstacles that are set against you that you have limited control over. However, you can control your tone. This does not mean changing who you are, but making little adjustments. It also doesn't mean you have to change how you approach things.

Even for himself as a man, when John first started teaching, he would project his voice above everybody else, until it was suggested to him by some teachers it was actually more effective if he lowered his voice. When he made the change, it automatically got students' attention. He also recalls, how he has had to adapt to the culture of his environment in other manners as well.

To further illustrate this point, John points out that even Margaret Thatcher learnt to adapt her image, by lowering the pitch of her voice so as not to sound bossy. She also had to make some changes to her appearance in order to be more acceptable to a wider audience. John clarifies that this requirement is not unique to female politicians, as even Tony Blair and Barack Obama had to make some adjustments to become more acceptable.

Young Women

Thinking of young women entering and trying to navigate the work environment, John emphasises the need for them to be observant. He speaks of the need to smile more and speak less with the aim of understanding who you're dealing with because there is more to people than meets the eye. He advises "listen to the small comments that are often important. Don't get involved in things that may appear political. Most important of all, observe what is going on around you." He further emphasises that it is important to know that at times the workplace can be like a battlefield.

Thinking specifically of women of colour, John recommends that they have someone outside of their workplace that they can trust who can mentor them. It could be someone of the same gender, but most important is that you can trust them and you know that they have your best interest at heart.

Bringing About Change

John believes it would be ideal for men to be more understanding of women, however, there are men that see women as a threat as most organisational hierarchies are in the shape of a pyramid with limited opportunities as you progress. As a result, unless organisations become less hierarchical with a focus on valuing and rewarding people whatever they do within the work environment there will be a limited number of men open to support the progression of women.

There are, however, men who will be willing to support women regardless and women need to identify those men within their organisations. If women can identify men that don't see women as a threat or competition then such men will be able to help women understand and navigate the environment. Such men will also generally advocate for women.

Though unsure how it would come about, John believes that more open dialogue would also be useful to bring about change.

Microbusinesses – Micropower

Colin Crooks is a Social Entrepreneur who works across sectors to address significant social and environmental issues. He currently runs Tree Shepherd, which enables business start-ups in disadvantaged communities in order to raise ambition, create employment and reduce inequality by tapping into the talents and passions of residents and businesses in the local area.

Colin works with people running small or micro-businesses, most of whom are self-employed. At the time that I spoke to him, 85% of the people Colin was working with were women, 80% from ethnic minority backgrounds, 25% had a disability or long term illness and more than one fifth were single parents.

An Entrepreneurial Journey

Colin has been a Social Entrepreneur since he was 30 years old. He is driven by his preoccupation with the environment and his concerns about unemployment; coupled with the belief that unemployment is a desperate waste of people. Over time, he has set up a number of recycling companies for which he had to employ over one thousand people. In the process, he met several people whose lives have been very different from his, people who were striving against the odds. In helping them to move from unemployment into employment, he found that they were all loyal and more productive than the average person once they were given time to acclimatise to the work environment. He also found them to be fun to work with. Colin's most recent recycling businesses closed in 2011 following the financial recession. Reappraising what he was doing and listening to several people he employed talk about their dreams, Colin decided that rather than look to employ people in another factory type of setting, he would help them to create their own businesses. Things kicked off when he wrote a short advertisement for a training programme and put it up in the library. Demonstrating the huge interest in self-employment, 29 people turned up and everything developed from there.

Women's Participation

As to the reason why more women than men tend to participate in his programmes, Colin doesn't believe he can speak with certainty, however, he has two instincts:

As Colin generalises, men are more inclined to get on with things without stopping to go on a structured course. Colin himself has only done a limited amount of formal business training, but has learnt the hard way, making mistakes along the way and losing his thick long hair in the process because of the stressful way in which he approached things. For instance, in his first five years, he was unaware of, and therefore did not use, cash flow forecast. Eventually learning about that was transformational.

Secondly, Colin believes women tend to be much more conservative and risk-averse. This may be because, as in the case of a number of the women he works with, they have caring responsibilities, both for parents and children. As such, Colin thinks there is a natural conservativism of women who have the responsibility for nurturing and caring. Colin refers to the old trope about men going out to hunt, coming home to the women who do the cooking. Women still typically have the caring responsibilities even if they work outside the home, while men still have the freedom to go out and do other things, with failure having fewer consequences. Colin believes this is a deep underlying truth that still has an impact. Women therefore want the support and reassurance that what they are doing will work.

Women's Approach

When men network, as you see in the City of London, there is often a focus on exchanging business cards, selling and getting business. Tree Shepherd teaches that networking is about getting to know people and building trust between individuals. Women are very good at this as they more naturally tend to network with a focus on getting to know people, developing an understanding about their lives and building relationships and so they should not be intimidated or put off from networking. Colin believes that the fact that Tree

Shepherd's approach to networking aligns naturally to women's networking approach is part of what draws women to the organisation.

Women tend to be happier sharing personal problems they encounter such as juggling two children during the school run and running a crochet business. Even though such things may impact the running of his business, Colin, as a man ,would only share such things with very close friends. He has noticed and finds it interesting that women, however, seem to feel more comfortable talking to casual acquaintances about such things, exchanging quite detailed information about things such as their children in conversation.

Coin believes this is immensely constructive as it helps to build trust. In leadership training you are taught of the importance of building trust with your team and other people. To do so you need to expose some of your vulnerabilities. He believes men find this much harder to do than women.

If women get the balance right without overdoing it, this can make it easier for them to develop strong teams and therefore better outcomes. He believes there does, however, need to be a balance with sharing information at work, most especially if a woman is in charge. It can become a problem if a manager is at one moment telling people off and in the next moment sharing details about her personal life. Colin believes there needs to be some separation. Men would do well to share more, while women might do so less. The further downside of this is if a supplier was to tell a buyer that they had problems at home and that was affecting production, it could invalidate her business and the buyer might be worried about buying from her. Colin believes there is a need to build trust without sharing your weaknesses.

The Tree Shepherd Model

Tree Shepherd works to a seven stage progression model:

Stage One: I want to run a business

Stage Two: Developing and starting a Business Model

Stage Three: Starting to sell to strangers which is a big transition point as you have someone you don't know valuing what you do enough to pay for it.

You move from Stage Four through to Six as the business develops and then on to Stage Seven which is employing people.

The men on the programme tend to get to Stage Three relatively more quickly than the women and then stop attending once they've reached this stage. On the other hand, the women take longer to progress, requesting one-to-one support sessions or other additional support. They take more time to get to stage three and then to move on up the stages, engaging much more in the learning. A lot of the women don't tend to scale up and grow their businesses as the men are more inclined to. The women are more likely to reach a comfort (if not confident) stage that they are happy with and continue to run their business at that level.

Constraints

At times Colin encounters women who are constrained by challenges at home such as limited space to work, domestic abuse, managing childcare while working and sometimes the challenge of reaching the threshold that would prevent them from claiming Housing Benefits while lacking sufficient income to cover housing costs. The system can be extremely abusive in that manner.

Women may also be limited in developing and growing a business as they are not always quick to self-promote. Typically, if a man's product is 80%, it's good enough for him; a woman will want her offering to be perfect, yet perfect is the enemy of good and stops them from trading. The time it takes to try to get a product to perfection may also make is more expensive or limit the women's profit.

Opportunity

A lot of the businesses are in areas such as sewing, crafts, crochet, mosaics and about 20% catering businesses with food from all across the world. The women are often running their businesses in parallel to the role of homemaker, providing them with a good balance between looking after their families and earning an income. It also provides them with a much more convenient and practical option than trying to take on a part time job to complement their caring responsibilities which would often require a number of hours' travel, if they can actually get a job that complements their children's school hours.

Strength & Response

R ob Neil OBE was born to Jamaican parents who moved to England in the 1960s. Formerly the Head of Culture Change & Leadership at the Department for Education, having worked previously within the UK Ministry of Justice for 36 years, Rob is now the Director at Krystal Alliance, a consultancy supporting organisations to be more inclusive. He was also the Chair of the Civil Service Race Forum from 2001-03 and 2016-18. He was a founding member of the REACH Society through which black male Role Models mentor and coach students in schools and universities across the UK.

The Value of Women at Work

Rob was interviewed by two women to join the Civil Service. Through his 37 year years within the service he has worked with different women in various capacities. On the value that women bring to the workplace, speaking in general terms, Rob finds women to be instinctively more collaborative and more capable of displacing their ego, putting what they might personally want to one side, to achieve and deliver for the benefit of the wider team. Rob adds that this does not apply to all women, but generally applies to those who are operating with their authentic self. There are also those who tend to mimic and ape the alpha-male leadership style, even down to their dressing. Sadly, this may at times extend to women responding viciously toward other women when it comes to personal requests for things such as maternity leave. Rob saw this exemplified in a woman who was not herself a parent, having no affinity or understanding of another woman's requests as a parent. More generally, though, Rob describes women as having an instinctive and more sensitive approach to what is needed to work through any kind of crisis. Rob mentions that this is highlighted in reports around the COVID-19 pandemic with nations such as New Zealand and others led by women doing best in managing the pandemic. Against this backdrop, he believes it is sad that there are so few women on FTSE100 company Boards.

Women's Impact on Their Progression

Rob believes there are several factors that affect whether women get into some roles and their limited progression within organisations despite what they have to offer. The most immediate factor, he says, is women themselves. This is not to shift the blame from men, but it is to say he has seen several women suffer because they focused on gaps they perceived in what they were able to do rather than concentrating on what they can do. Rob exemplifies, in his experience from coaching and mentoring, numerous men and women over the years. Each may apply for a job requiring six competencies. Both the man and the woman have a competence they're not skilled in but the woman will withhold her application because she hasn't got that competency. The man will go for it anyway with the view of finding a way to catch up. Rob finds he needs to encourage women to apply anyway, as 'you've got to be in it to win it'.

Other Impacts on Women's Progression

Rob believes there are other factors as well. Men have designed the world for men and it is consequently hard-wired for men. Rob speaks of accessibility, using some of the examples highlighted in Caroline Criado Perez's book, 'Invisible Women'. It for example speaks of the standard size of a mobile phone which better fits the size of a man's hand, the ergonomics of a piano keyboard, of women's toilets in public spaces which apply parity in design with no thought about what different genders require and the resultant queues for women. Rob recommends Caroline's book and says it contains many other insightful examples e.g. the power of imagery and symbols such as statues and posters that are male driven and focused. Perhaps this contributes to why, as Rob says, there are also the things women tell themselves which sadly can encourage imposter syndrome.

Challenges and Opportunities of Black Women

Reflecting on the specific challenges and opportunities that may relate to black women, Rob speaks of how he has been surrounded by, brought up by and influenced by black Caribbean women, all beautiful, intelligent, hardworking and talented. Right now his life is surrounded by his wife who is from St Vincent, his best friend who is from Jamaica and his mum, also from Jamaica. He has gained great wisdom from them, and they have helped to inform and instil a certain work ethic in him. He also has an aunt who has been highly influential.

With black women, there is often a strong sense of being self-reliant and independent when getting things done. They have a tendency to see something that needs to be done and see it as the responsibility of the person in the mirror. There is a strength in this belief in getting things done. Rob can't say specifically whether this applies to other women at a personal level, but can speak of black women based on his personal experience.

On the impact of a strong, independent black woman in the work-place; that strength helps them to endure some of the micro-aggressions (i.e. the everyday occurrence of discrimination and racism they may face in the workplace). They see them, acknowledge them and move on from them saying this isn't me or what I deserve. Some-times they may then take action to deal with the situation. On other occasions they may disengage from the perpetrator on the basis that they only need to have limited exposure or contact with such behaviour. Others may more successfully find ways of nurturing relations and managing their environment.

Whether she responds in a manner in which people then see her as aggressive or she disengages, it is sad and shouldn't happen. To try to prevent this from happening, a number of people are working to ensure it doesn't. This is part of the role and power of BAME Staff Networks where many people are sharing their experiences, most recently as an additional effect of the attention to a global Black Lives Matter movement. Rob believes that black professional women are generally becoming better at learning how to play the game and becoming more supportive of each other. As a result they are making progress and moving into some very powerful positions based on their abilities and the support they provide to each other in navigating life's journey.

Playing The Game to Succeed

Rob believes that care has to be taken in trying to play the game as there is a risk of women suddenly waking up and realising that they have lost their identity in the process because they are no longer bringing their authentic self into situations. It's therefore dangerous to get caught up in a game, while the reality is we are all in a game. Black women therefore need to learn how to utilise their incredible strength effectively. They need to understand the system they are working within, while ensuring that they retain their identity.

Improving The Work World for Women

To improve the situation for women in the world of work, Rob believes we all, men and women alike, black or white, have a responsibility to study commensurate with our ambition. In the world that we live in, things by nature will not automatically land in the lap of the under-represented.

Rob emphasises that this is not a criticism and it doesn't mean that people born into privilege are not good people. The reality is that with class structures, monarchies and intergenerational wealth, there are people who will walk into situations with inherited advantages that place them ahead of other people. Right or wrong, this is reality. As a result, for black people in general, with whatever qualifications people may have, there is a need for us to study commensurate with our ambitions. Racism is a reality, but as Toni Morrison's says, as a function it is a distraction. We must remain focused. In that focus we must grow strong enough to speak truth to power, to recognise those moments when they occur, to seize them and learn how to make the most of them. As individuals, we need to build networks around us that provide us with safe spaces to earth our emotions. He adds that life is full of waves and we can help each other to be better surfers.

The COVID-19 Pandemic has had a disproportionate impact for people from Black, Asian and Ethnic Minority Communities. It's not that the virus is racist, however we know that co-morbidities and pre-existing conditions, which are exacerbated by institutional racism, render Black, Asian and Minority Ethnic Communities more susceptible and exposed to the virus.

When speaking about women of colour, Rob believes there is a specific need for people to come together to provide a particular strength to overcome the unique challenges faced.

Rob also highlights the insightful work of Jennifer Izekor at Above Difference, whose diversity work highlights the importance of combining cultural intelligence with emotional intelligence to better prepare us for the future demands of an ever increasingly diverse world. He explains this work enables people to better articulate the speech of their hearts, combined with the development of the capability to work across different cultures and describes it as an exciting potential for progressive transformational change. This leads back to the need for people to be prepared by studying commensurate with their ambition without allowing any oppressions endured to adversely impact the approach, but evolving to lead through whatever we may be faced with, with our best offering without feeling the need to be validated by others.

Some women may feel it is limiting to be their authentic self and risk not being accepted. However, Rob says it's actually liberating. He believes balance needs to be struck by women as others, concluding

"Our best self, our joy, is not in seeking superiority, but rather in simply being who we are and looking after ourselves as we journey in being all of who we are. That is our strength and beautiful response."

The Place & Space of a Queen

Jerome Harvey Agyei is a passionate and driven young man who grew up in the care system from the age of four. Jerome is a strong advocate for Children's Rights and a Participation Worker who supports young people in care. He currently works for the Violence Reduction Unit at the London Mayor's Office and is an Ambassador for One Young World.

Young Care Leavers

In Jerome's work, he uses his personal experience to bring home to professionals the feelings of young people in care and the experience of leaving care from the point of view of a child or young person. In doing so, he aims to minimise the hurdles young people face and make a real difference.

Thinking specifically about young women who have been in care who go into the work environment, based on his knowledge and observations, Jerome believes that their experiences of the world of work will partly depend on the individual and the meaning they've given to their experiences. On the positive side, women who have been in care will have developed resilience because they will have had to deal with trauma and the care system. When a woman has been in the care system and has had positive experiences then going into work, she is less likely to have the fear that most other young women would have going into an unfamiliar environment. She may therefore come with a level of resilience, confidence and a lack of fear. She's also likely to be able to meet goals and achieve her aspirations. Women that have been in care are often more nurturing, even though or perhaps because they have lacked nurture themselves. This makes them powerhouses.

On the contrary, some women have been disempowered by the care system and continue to feel completely disempowered. Getting into the workplace they may feel things are pointless as they haven't been able to identify the Queen within themselves and no one has told them they are Queens. This especially applies to those who have suffered sexual abuse, which has a major impact on a women's view of men. When you go into the world of work, it is often perceived that men run the world of work by virtue of their positions of power and this can be a trigger for a young woman who has been abused by men or observed them being abusive to others. This may leave her feeling even more disempowered. As a result, it's important to have women around who can model how to interact, while also being supportive and protective. It's also important that men are conscious and aware of some of the issues that may exist.

Sensitivity & Space to Understand

Though not always purposely, men often lack sensitivity to women's experiences. Jerome points to the fact that when you look at history, it is focused around 'HiStory' and not 'Her-Story' and told through male perspective of the world. Work has also been dominated by men in privileged positions. There is a need to acknowledge that there has been an imbalance. Times are changing; while there are some men that don't seem to want to see empowered women, there are men like Jerome who advocate for them and believe that this is the time for women to put their true, authentic and powerful selves forward and rise as Queens. Men don't always recognise how much women have held space for men and come up with important ideas. Jerome believes that now is the time to find the right balance between men and women. He believes that, for this change to come about, there is the need to have space for authentic conversations, which is something that he incorporates in his work. He believes there is a need for conversations about men's power and the power imbalance between men and women at work and in all other environments.

Yin and Yang

Jerome believes there is also a need for women to be engaged, not because they are beautiful and nice to look at (aesthetics), but because of what they have to offer, so that they can bring their authentic selves to the work environment. Expanding on the real value that women bring to the work environment, Jerome says that if you look at our nature, women are very nurturing while men are very logical, so they look at things differently. If you have an idea then it's good to have both a man's and women's perspective because they will always look at things differently. Being clear that he is generalising as it doesn't apply to all, Jerome mentions how women he works with analyse things differently and can put things in a way that moves people. They connect emotionally and can see the meaning behind things. He also finds some women to be smarter. They bring a feminine essence which is needed.

Jerome believes when you have men and women together, it's like Yin and Yang. In nature, you can't create life with just a male or female, you need both; it's the same with work. He believes you can't grow something without the essence of the masculine and feminine. Feminine energy and insight is important to Jerome at work. He finds women tend to question if things feels right. They are more inclined to check if it's aligned to the espoused values and questions what it actually means for the people and world around us. Women also bring a long-term perspective, rather than just thinking from the short-term. He believes you see a lot of this in work environments where there are mainly women such as the care sector.

Female Empowerment

Women themselves have a part to play in addressing the imbalance in the world of work. Jerome believes this process has already started with women standing up for their rights as seen with the #MeToo movement and the increased number of women standing for political positions to the extent that there is now a Women's Equality Party. Key is it needs to be about empowering women and not against men or anything else. Jerome would love to see a female empowerment event that men attend and just listen to how women feel without comment. He wants to see men watching women in dialogue without interrupting. He believes listening from the heart would provide men with a better understanding of the power and value women bring into any environment.

Jerome is aware there have always been women in the past in the forefront of thinking who are silent heroines because you don't typically hear much about them in history or religious books, rarely written from the female perspective. It would be valuable if there were more stories written about and from the female perspective that amplify the female voice for future generations.

Men confident in their own worth should not feel afraid of empowered women, but should celebrate them as a requirement for the balance of life. Women should be able to be who they are (as should men). Jerome believes that if we give women the chance, the amount of solutions and problems that will be achieved would be amazing. Jerome believes there would be less destruction in the world with more female leaders, as they would have the attitude of not wanting to harm or kill children. He believes a lot of positive change happens when women are in charge.

Queens

Jerome calls women Queens because although he doesn't understand how it feels, he believes what women have to deal with is mind blowing. As they physically create life, it means they are the closest thing to God. They have to go through a major amount of pain in order to give birth. Once a month their entire body changes because of hormones that may cause imbalances which they can't control. Not only do they hold space for men but if they have one, they hold space for a child while they're also trying to be the best person they can be for that child. Women then typically show up for a partner and additionally do whatever is they do on a day-to-day basis. This to Jerome makes women Queens.

Unfortunately, females are at times seen as trophies and this puts no value on a woman as it's all sexual. If females realised they were Queens, they would refuse to compromise their values to impress men who they really mean nothing to. Also, if men valued women as Queens, they would be clear that women don't need to compromise their values to impress them. Jerome therefore calls women Queens as he knows they hold a special space and energy, a royal status.

Beacon Queens

There are a few women that Jerome highlights as Queens who stand out as beacons for other women. First is his biological mum who has been through so much trauma and pain, but has managed it all and continues to make progress in life. His foster mum who very much helped him to become the person he is today by teaching him some crucial underlying values. She loves unconditionally and in doing so she has given Jerome the gift of love that has a ripple effect; he believes now that he has received that gift, he can give it out to other people. He especially remembers his foster mum telling him to always read the small print, not just on documents, but the print of life. Everyone you meet comes with small print, so when you meet people and their behaviour is not what you would expect, you need to realise they have a small print that differs from what you might expect that affects how they behave. You therefore need to build an understanding of people via their small print.

Then, there's Jerome's friend Shalyce, who has an incredible amount of wisdom. She is the most nurturing and confident person you can speak to and have an authentic conversation with. She is also a skilled listener.

Jerome also mentions Kate Gledhill, an absolute Queen who holds space for the whole care community. She knows and taught Jerome how to communicate with people in a loving and caring manner when he was doing his training.

Outside of the women that Jerome knows personally, he also mentions Michelle Obama, a very accomplished woman in her own right who stood behind her husband, Barack Obama, throughout his presidency. Michelle has always seemed more interesting to Jerome than Barack Obama. Although she has also been a major part of history, Obama will be the person spoken about in history and not Michelle. Jerome believes with the Obamas, that Barack does however not only demonstrate listening to a woman but also how to respect and honour a woman in the way he talks about her and says he would not have achieved what he had without her. Jerome finds Michelle to be powerful, honest real and authentic. She is in such a privileged and powerful place, yet you can still relate to her.

Jerome highlights all the women he mentions have a very nurturing and loving energy on top of everything else. They're also very much in tune with their energy, intuition and feelings.

For Young Women

For a young woman entering and trying to navigate the world of work, Jerome says:

"Know who you are. You are royalty, you are a Queen. Embrace who you are without expectations from anyone else and know you can do anything if you take the time to rise. Now is a good time to rise and so do yourself the service of stepping up to be what you want to be. Understand that you are valuable. If you understand how powerful you are, then the world is your oyster."

Specifically, for the young female who is care experienced or has been through some other form of trauma:

"You might not know it, but you are already a warrior; you're already a Queen. You've already overcome so you're really strong. You may not always feel great, but invest in healing and understanding that you are a powerful person even though your experience in life to date may not have been good to you. Once you have a clear mind, you will you will be better able to define who you want to be. Invest in yourself and don't let external factors define who you are."

The Care System

When children and young people cannot be properly looked after and cared for at home, they are taken into the care of the State. In the vast majority of cases this is in no way the fault of the child or young person. The system is referred to as the Care Leavers and such young people are described as being in care; care leavers when they reach the age of independence.

In 2018 there were close to 100,000 in the United Kingdom's Care System.

Features of Success

S am Onigbanjo is a Digital Marketing and
Communications Specialist. Sam is also co-founder
alongside his wife, Tola of Women4Africa, a Global
Cultural organisation formed in 2011 to celebrate African
women and their contribution to society. Women4Africa
recognises and celebrate women often unrecognised; the
highly visible platform is designed to empower and
showcase African women as major contributors to global
development.

Women4Africa

Women4Africa came about when Sam and his wife decided to develop
a business idea that they could work on together. Sam has a passion
for building African communities, while his wife Tola has a passion
for women. This led them to think of African women from the perspective of African women both in African and across the world in the
diaspora inclusive of women who are not black, but were born in
Africa. They decided to find a way of not just celebrating African

194

women, but also of empowering them. This came with Sam's realisation that effective African Leadership was impossible without women. Sam further explains that women give birth to men. If there were no women, there would be no men. If you think of all the success trophies that a man may have, his partner is always the most important, regardless of how many Ferraris or other possessions he may own. This made Women4Africa and his wife's interest in women a compelling project for Sam.

Ten years on from the setup of Women4Africa, at the most basic of levels it has provided African women with the opportunity to network with women of African heritage globally, leading to collaborations. It has also enabled young people in the diaspora to connect more with their African heritage and culture. Additionally, it has created a greater sense of pride in Africa. Women4Africa has also created role models and inspiration for women when they see the profiles of those who win awards from Women4Africa. At a personal level, Sam is finding it very fulfilling and feels as if he's building a real legacy. Sam also loves the opportunity it has provided for him to work in partnership with his wife, which brings the opportunity to gain a greater appreciation of the stunning skills she has which differ completely from his. He highlights that she has phenomenal interpersonal skills and attention to detail; she counts every single thing almost to the hairs on your head. He finds this awe inspiring.

The Value of Women

Speaking more generally about the value that women and most especially African women, bring to the work environment, Sam talks about growing up with his mother who was a very hardworking woman who made hard work a norm to him. Now retired, his mum was a Fashion Designer. He recalls coming home from school and walking into her studio to see her and members of her staff cutting away at materials and sitting down to attend to customers. Coming from such an environment, he believes gender is irrelevant to people's ability to work hard and he engages with people based on their merit and ability to do a good job rather than their gender.

Sam has observed both the positive and not so positive things that women bring to the workplace. He re-emphasises the attention to detail he has seen in his wife as a feature that also applies to other women. He finds them to be extremely supportive. He also believes that there are some very intelligent women, often more intelligent than men, no matter how intelligent a man may be. Men need to be able to tap into this, he says. He has noticed that such women are often happy to be second in charge. It can be highly beneficial to work with a very clever woman if you understand the value she brings and listen to her feedback. You'll find her feedback to be critical. Sam finds it difficult to understand why such capable women may feel timid about speaking in public with the level of knowledge they have. Instead, he finds himself in situations where they provide him with solutions and he ends up speaking up or asserting a point. He sees this as real added value.

He does believe that women at times allow their emotions to get in the way and they would do better if they better managed them. He mentions that if a group of women have a disagreement, they seem to find it difficult to let go of the problem. Sam believes this may be a barrier to leadership for some women regardless of all of their gifts. It's difficult to manage people if you can't manage your emotions, he asserts.

Sam doesn't believe there is anything wrong with women forging ahead and taking the lead. There will, however, be people that have negative perceptions about you whether you're male or female and such people may try to trip you up. This happens to men as well and it can come from males or female; it's not always about gender. Sometimes they are simply not pleasant people and just don't want others to succeed. It's important for women not to get caught up with their emotions and get stuck in such situations. They need to learn to manage such the situation.

Paradigms

As much as women may be limited because they don't put themselves forward and may take things personally, letting their emotions get in the way, Sam identifies societal bias as an external factor to women's progression. There are men that may not appreciate what women can do. If you speak to people, you may find they have other reasons for their biases, right or wrong. On a personal level, there are men who believe that if your wife earns more than them, she's going to start bossing them around. In order to try to prevent this, they try to suppress their wives. Not because they hate them, but because they see it as a way of preserving their home. There are also men that may have previously been hurt by a woman. Because of an experience of having been wounded by a woman, such men may go on to see women as aggressors and react to women on those basis. That, says, Sam is such a man's narrative and his truth which he may carry with him and bases his life on. It's very hard, but what do you say to him as that's his truth? As much as it is a challenge it is his paradigm. In Sam's option, the work environment is a reflection of society, so it's likely that what he does at work is what he does at home as well.

A man's experiences, assumptions and therefore paradigms may affect how he engages with women at work. It is innate in people to treat others on the basis of whatever tendencies they may have. If for instance, you have a person with vicious tendencies, you need to remove those tendencies for the person to stop treating people viciously on the basis of their gender, ethnicity or whatever bias they may have. You can't just look at it as an issue of ethnicity or gender for this behaviour.

Sam does not agree with such behaviour and wouldn't support it. He, however, recognises that he may only have limited influence over such a person. He highlights the need for effective leadership for such people. If an organisation is led by such a person, it is in a lot of trouble and such a person needs help. There is crucially something deeper going on inside of someone that leads them to oppress others.

In considering the way forward, Sam emphasise the importance of being a bit more loving and kind to others. This he believes will begin to reduce the extent to which people are judged on the basis of their gender, race or sexuality. If women don't take care, they risk absorbing the behaviour of men who have mistreated them and may end up taking out their frustration on other men lower down in an organisation's hierarchy who have done nothing wrong. Unleashing hell on such a guy may lead him to develop his own negative paradigms such as not wanting a female boss because of the way he was treated, leading to a cycle which means change does not happen and the negative behaviour goes on and on.

Sam believes that regardless of how a woman may have been treated, there is a need for her to try to understand where the person in question is coming from, to try to remain positive so as not to become negative and start treating other people badly, continuing the chain.

Award Winning Characteristics

Characterising the women who tend to receive awards for Women4-Africa, Sam finds they typically have a simplicity and/or humility about them no matter their achievement level, whilst being very kind, incredibly aspirational women who want to go on to another level to achieve more.

Simplicity & Kindness

Whether they are women that are at the top of the ladder, PhD holders, struggling to make ends meet or as with one, a billionaire, they always have a humanitarian or philanthropic activity they are involved in and want to do more. They are never too busy to find time to offer their support for a cause or a need.

The Spirit of Aspiration

Sam highlights the case of the CEO of a PLC in her early fifties. She has already achieved so much yet she speaks of how she's only just begun and wants to build a conglomerate and help other people. She's already wealthy and could very easily shut her door and say goodbye to everything else. At the other end of the spectrum, Sam speaks of a woman in her late thirties living in a council flat, on shaky footing, but still willing to share what she has to help others.

Allying with Good Men

To achieve success, women need to be able to recognise that not all women are on their side and not all men are against them. If they work in organisations with the right men in charge, they are going to do exactly what the women want them to do. Sam believes there are a lot of men like him that do the right thing for both men and women and do not accept inequality for any reason. They have a different paradigm. For Sam this stems from being brought up by a strong woman. The image in his mind when it comes to women, is "I'm not letting anyone suppress my mum". So in any environment he will always give women an equal opportunity.

It may be a numbers game in which women may have to keep knocking on doors and be prepared to kiss a few ugly frogs in order to find men that are right to support, guide, mentor and work beside them. Sam has always thought positively about women, but people may not have been aware of this until he had the platform of Women4Africa. Without the platform, people could be unaware and may have had a negative view of him. Women therefore need to take an open approach and keep on until they are fortunate enough to meet the right men. There is something about the way Barack Obama interacts with his wife, Michelle that leads Sam to believe that he is the type of man he's talking about. Being brought up by his mother, a strong figure, and his grandma, means he's likely to have that sort of capital. Sam believes there are a lot of people like that; they just need to be identified.

The Next Generation

Going forward, Women4Africa is expanding to run digital seminars to empower teenagers and young women. To further help teenaged girls enhance their value, he believes it is important for them to have a plethora of mentors who can speak to them and they need to consider what they are being told. It will help them to progress faster, making fewer mistakes and to be more productive in life. They need to start by painting a picture of what they really want their life to be like. He believes in that way they will know how to identify the wrong type of mentors who may seem right, but are not. That will leave them room to listen to the right ones. There are two voices out there, says Sam. One sounds good and is terrible and one that isn't so obvious but is really good for them. This is all important for young people, but equally applies to women at any stage in their career.

Women4Africa award nominees and award winners is a good place to look for female mentors. The organisation also has some incredible members of staff with hearts of gold who are always willing to help.

A Pro-Feminist Approach

Randy Agyemang was born in Germany and described his background as African-European. In his early twenties, he is currently studying for a BA in Architecture at Manchester School of Architecture. He's also done work as a School Technician, Bar Worker, Model and Retail Assistant. He is a supporter of the homeless and previously slept homeless for a week in Manchester in order to raise awareness and money for local charities. He is an avid advocate for Social Justice.

Whilst at University, Randy's primary focus is on studying, while additionally doing some bar work, modelling and event planning. While Randy has worked with more men than women in management positions, he's definitely seen differences with men and women in the workplace.

Valuing Women in Management

Randy believes that although there are more women in management positions than there used to be he has noticed a difference in their roles in comparison to men. Men in management seem to be able to take more of a laid-back approach as one of the boys. Women on the other hand seem to have to have more of a stern exterior in order to get the equal respect of their male counterparts. Randy believes this is even more so for women of colour who it seems are often undermined in the workplace. Women generally (most especially women of colour) seem to have to work harder and definitely face more barriers. There is also a question in Randy's mind as to whether women are always recruited because they are seen as the best people for a job or whether it's to tick a box to say there is some diversity in place from the perspective of the decision makers. This is because they often seem to get the management roles, but they don't give always seem to be given the same level of respect as their male counterparts.

Contemplating the value that women typically bring to the work environment, Randy refers back to his first manager when he worked in retail for Clark Shoes. His manager was a woman who brought a maternal element to work which made him feel a lot more valued. He generally finds women to be more empathetic and sympathetic. He believes that they are more caring and bring more concern to the workplace with the best interests of their team at heart. Unfortunately they sometimes seem to feel undermined in their roles with the need to assert themselves. Randy sympathises with women in these circumstances and can understand them behaving in this manner so as not to be sexualised but be respected at work.

Intergenerational Attitudes towards Women

Randy believes this may be a reflection of social norms of earlier generations when women's roles in the workplace were limited. It's only now that women have started gaining some status in the workplace, but he believes a lot of the attitudes towards women have been transferred from one generation to the next and a number of men treat people on the basis of the attitudes and behaviours of their fathers and grandfathers. Randy also sees this reflected by the media and in old films and TV shows.

Randy sees this reflected with awards where the Best Architect and business Mogul awards typical go to white men. Architecture is still very much male dominated, where the presence of women is still limited.

Gender Stereotyped Careers

Randy believes women are just as talented as men. He believes they should be encouraged from a young age to take up whatever career they want inclusive of areas such as architecture and not just limit themselves to roles that are traditionally seen as roles for women such as nursing (unless it's what they are passionate about and really want). Randy believes that education at times pushes people towards gendered roles right from primary education. When different careers are discussed in schools, nurses are normally depicted by women, while the doctors and scientist are depicted by men. Randy points out, if you keep seeing this type of imagery from a young age it eventually becomes your perceived reality. Even in history, although there have been some great female scientists over time, they are often forgotten.

The Visibility of Women in Architecture

In Architecture, there are plenty of women doing great work, however, very few are spoken about with the exception of Zaha Hadid, the best-known and celebrated female Architect in the world who passed away in 2016. Randy has not noticed that even in the case of Hadid with all of her achievements, numerous men will be mentioned before her name comes up in conversation. Hadid's recognition may have been aided by virtue of her education as she went to a number of private architecture schools including the prestigious Architecture Association which is similar to if she had gone to Eton or Cambridge. It is more difficult for other women to be visible and appreciated in a very male dominated environment.

Randy speaks of a meeting he attended with a female colleague who had led on the project. The client was not prepared to recognise her role in the project until he (Randy) insisted that the project could not proceed without her involvement, especially as he felt he was being credited for her exceptional work. He believes the challenge was enhanced as his colleague was from an ethnic minority back-ground. Randy does, however, believe there are professions that are more welcoming and open to women. He further believes it would help the Architectural profession if more women were recognised and received Awards. The celebration of women's successes in the profession would have a trickle down effect, because new generations of women at primary and secondary levels would see women in such positions and it would raise their aspirations about what they can achieve.

Male Voice and Support

The good thing is that younger people in the profession are more accepting and understanding of the issues. However, to move further forward, Randy believes that men should use their voice to vocalise injustices against women when they see them. It may even be that men being offered an award say that it should go to a woman who has done equally good if not better work. He asserts that the more educated and aware men are of the issues in relation to women's equality, the more they can actively encourage it. If we start to celebrate the value of women now, most especially amongst younger generations, it will become a societal norm.

Men on their own part need to value women more, placing equal value on their voices and treating women the same as their male counterparts when it comes to opportunities and promotion. He emphasises the need for men to encourage women to pursue careers in whatever industry they want to work in, even if it's not the norm.

Randy believes it's the responsibility of men just as much as women to improve and change things. Being ignorant does not help. Men need to become aware and to amplify their own voices in support of women and ensure they don't have to settle for less.

Men need to see women as their equals and understand their value, not just mentally, but by putting it into their actions and living it on a day to day basis. Even when no one else is watching or listening.men need to live by it.

Women's Perceived Aggression

If all responsibility is left in the hands of women, most especially black women, at times they may be forced to assert themselves in their bid to gain respect with the risk of coming across as aggressive. On the other hand, if a woman generally feels oppressed and does not assert herself (with the associated risk of being perceived as aggressive), she may end up being ignored or undermined. Her assertiveness may therefore be her only way of amplifying her voice to be heard if no one else stands up for her. It's unfortunate that at times this creates a negative stigma. It becomes much easier for women if they have the support of men around them.

To Young Women

To a young woman navigating her way into the world of work, Randy would say:

"Don't be discouraged. There will be barriers along the way, but just keep your heart strong and keep pushing, most especially in the current climate. Put your passion into whatever you want to do and pursue it. You might get knocked down a couple of times, but keep going, knowing that there will be people there to support you."

Men on Board with Gender Equality

R ick Zednik is is an independent consultant who until recently served as Managing Director of Women Political Leaders (WPL), the global network of female politicians aimed at increasing the number and influence of women who serve as national legislators, cabinet ministers, prime ministers and presidents. Rick has also worked in other senior level roles from which he has gained global experience. Rick is a values-driven leader committed to developing inclusive environments that thrive through the input of diverse perspectives.

Representation

Rick has believed for a long time that democracy operates best when it's truly representative of the citizenry. Any democracy that is not doing this in any respect simply can't be fully representing the interests of all of its constituents. For as long as policies and laws are made by politicians who are disproportionately over representing any segment of the population, this is going to be a problem. A problem which affect not just the people who are under represented and tend to be those who suffer the most, but also for those who are over-represented. As an able-bodied, straight, middle class, educated, white man from a Christian background, Rick is aware that he comes from a position of being overrepresented in almost all definitions. He does not believe he has suffered from any sort of disadvantages that he can think of except that he hasn't been able to benefit from a more holistic society where everybody's views are equally respected, represented and valued. He further believes that if he had more colleagues who were from all sorts of different backgrounds, he would have benefited from different ideas, fresh perspectives and, as a result, better decisions. This was key to Rick's decision to work for Women Political Leaders, something he did for four years. Rick strongly believes that if we at last address the imbalance in relation to gender, we will have better political decisions in our society and this makes for a better society for everybody.

During the early stages of the COVID-19 Pandemic, Rick wrote on how several male political leaders' response to COVID-19 was to talk about it as a battle as if they were going to war against some sort of enemy. Rick thought this was fundamentally misguided because it is not war; there is not an enemy that was going to attack us in any militarily conventional way. Thinking of it in such terms could lead to the making of bad decisions because it's a totally different set of chal-lenges. There isn't an enemy making decisions as there would be in a military conflict. Rick believes that, as such, we need to think about the pandemic in totally different terms with the requirement for people to come together.

Gender influence on the Covid Pandemic

Rick is a dual citizen of the United States of America and Slovakia, with one parent from each country. These two countries have dealt with the pandemic in totally different ways, with a male and female leader, respectively. At the early stage of the pandemic, there were State Governors in America competing against each other to buy ventilators and other equipment. Rick believes there should have been supplies going where they were most needed, rather than to people who could afford to pay the highest price. On the other hand, there was another type of leader, mainly women, who took a more collective approach. They didn't speak in the I or Me or focus on themselves or any individuals, but instead focused on the collective group. They tended to take a more collaborative than competitive approach. Resources were distributed based on where they might do the greatest good for the greatest numbers.

Rick also found that the female leaders took more of a coaching approach, as opposed to a commanding approach. Rick illustrates this contrast with the example of the male Prime Minister of Great Britain on television instructing people that they must stay at home. Prime Minister Jacinda Arden of New Zealand, on the other hand, acted earlier and spoke of what everyone needed to do and spoke of how everyone should look out for each other in a way that made it feel that people had in interest in protecting themselves and those around them, as opposed to people feeling they were being issued commands.

While recognising that it is a generalisation, Rick believes that the differences in male and female approaches that can be seen in the political sphere can also be observed in the workplace. Women Political Leaders is an organisation whose staff is mainly female. He found it to be much more collaborative, with a lot more cheerleading than other places he's worked. It even comes across in little things, such as how people typically thank others. This also makes it often more harmonious than other work environments, even if it's not always the most efficient. In the cultures of other organisations where Rick has worked, women may adapt more to the prevailing culture as opposed to the situation in Women Political Leaders, which was created by females. Typically, people try to conform to the culture of the organisation they are working in. As such, women in a culture which has rules set by men will typically have to try to conform to that culture in order to succeed.

Barriers in the Workplace

Reflecting on the barriers that women often face in the workplace, Rick believes there are two broad categories of hindrances to women: other people and themselves. Rick has done a lot of hiring over the years in different organisations in different countries. He's noticed the people doing the hiring often want to get results without spending a lot of time on the process. Often people get a pool of candidates who are not particularly diverse in terms of gender or other dimensions, but don't keep looking for a more diverse pool of candidates because they believe they've done what they are supposed to and don't have time to keep looking.

In addition, there are often unfair assumptions made about male and female candidates. There may be a female candidate who is very accomplished and impressive. However, because of the expectation that she's not going to stay in the job for the next five to ten years as she's most likely going to take a break to spend time with family, an organisation often concludes that they can't afford to take her on. This is at times said overtly, but more often more dangerously, things just happen quietly or even unconsciously. These assumptions are hardly ever made about male candidates. Women themselves can't control this, but they're suffering from that unfair bias. Rick believes there is a requirement for cultures and systems to change to break this down and combat it.

Admitting to generalising, Rick believes that women may at times also not help themselves by not being as self-promoting as men are and suffer from this. It hinders their ability to progress or to get what they deserve, whether it's a certain pay level or responsibilities. Rick believes that until they advocate for themselves in equal measures to their male counterparts, it's going to be very difficult for them to get everything their males are getting. Simply said: if you don't ask, you don't get.

Men's Receptiveness to Feminism

Going beyond the hindrances highlighted above, there is a need for men's involvement to increase gender equality. Rick has previously written an article about getting men on board with gender equality. As in the article, he speaks of men in five categories based on their receptiveness to feminism:

OPPONENTS	SCEPTICS	UNCOMMITTED	SUPPORTERS	CHAMPIONS
Hard to convince, however, keep exposing them to positive messages	Happy with that status quo, may be coaxed to see things differently over time	Open-minded, but uncommitted, may attend the odd conference or event	Happy to support the cause, but may need some guidance on the how	Convinced and set on convincing others

At one end are the **Opponents.** It's hardly worth even trying to change their minds. To make changes in society, it's best to focus on the things that are changeable. It's not to say that opponents should be fully ignored as they are part of society and have an impact on what happens, but Rick does not believe it's worth spending a lot of energy with them. Instead, focus more on the other four categories.

Next on the spectrum are the **Sceptics.** While they have their own views, they are tolerant of other views and willing to engage in a conversation and listen a bit to what others have to say, unlike opponents who probably won't do much listening.

The third category is the **Uncommitted.** They are probably not vocal; however, they are very open-minded. They are the least set in an opinion one way or another and as a result, they are worth a lot of time and energy to be brought round to being receptive to feminism.

The fourth category are **Supporters.** They are convinced and believe feminism is a good thing and women deserve everything that men deserve. They don't believe it's strange to see women as leaders, even though they may not necessarily be openly vocal about it. As such, they support quietly; they are not going to lead the charge for change.

The fifth category are **Champions.** They don't just openly talk about change; they walk the walk and are really out there trying to persuade others.

Why Men Should Support Women

Rick presents two main arguments to encourage men to become supporters, if not outright champions of women in the workplace. In the first instance, it is just what's fair. Women should be given every opportunity that men are. If you expect it for yourself as a man, why is there any reason for you not to expect it for your sister, wife, daughter or any other women. It's just right for everyone to receive the same opportunity.

His second argument is much more based on self-interest. There is a fallacy that it's a zero-sum game in the workplace; that if I allow women the same opportunities as men, there is potentially going to be a negative result for me. We should all be able to compete as there is always a degree of competition in life, most certainly in work. If you have a competitor, you have to be as good as or better, with the best ideas. You need to have the best perspective so that you can make sure that you're attracting the best people to work for your organisation to get the best results. For any individual to thrive in their job, they need their organisation to do well, so they should want their organisation to benefit from different perspectives in order to attract good people and sell more to customers or whatever they do. Having the best people around you also provides you with the opportunity to grow personally.

Rick believes that if on the other hand, you're just surrounded by people who went to the same schools that you did and grew up in the same place that you did, you're going to be narrow-minded. It's only by interacting with people who have completely different experiences from ourselves that we expand our horizons and grow.

Recommendations to Women

For women trying to make progress in the workplace, Rick believes there is a need for them to recognise that while there will be setbacks and barriers, there is a need for women to keep working at what they want to achieve and know that nobody who ultimately gets anywhere does it by themselves, they do it thanks to others. They don't however, get there only because of others; they also get there because they have been persistent and kept at it.

214

Epilogue – Challenges of a Patriarchal Based Society

I believe there is no better way to conclude than to share some of the reflections of a 16 year old young man. In my dialogue with him, he spoke extensively about the patriarchal nature of society and how it manifest and impacts on different areas of society, feeding from education into the workplace and our lives as a whole. For all that has been achieved to date, his reflections really highlight how much still needs to change for women's value to be truly realised in the work environment. Due to his young age, I have not identified the 16 year old I spoke to by name and simply refer to him as Simon.

Expectations & Acceptance

Simon believes the desire to fit in as part of community and be accepted often leads children in school to adhere to particular expected sets of personality traits. If young people don't fit in, there often comes a fear of being vulnerable. While it's possible to get on without being accepted, it's harder to do so. He explains it's like raising yourself versus being part of a family.

Based on Simon's observations, gender expectations have not

changed much from what he's heard existed in earlier decades to the current day i.e. there is an expectation that girls are attractive; not too dumb, but not too smart either, physically weaker than boys and somewhat submissive so that boys are not intimidated or concerned that a girl will exceed them. This can be as superficial as a girl being taller than a boy being seen as a freak or odd. This is also embedded in the expectation for boys to be dominant in all fields except for domestic responsibilities.

Simon believes this is how our society was defined hundreds of years ago without much change. As a result, boys are still largely geared towards studying Science, Technology, Engineering and Mathematics (STEM) related subjects, basically anything that is logic-based. Girls on the other hand are encouraged to study subjects which are more essay based. As a result he is one of only four boys out of the thirty students in his Sociology class. He finds it odd that while boys are not encouraged to study writing based subjects, writing jobs seem to be dominated by men.

More generally, Simon believes there is an expectation for boys to show no signs of weakness and to be masculine, to be practical, to be less intangible, and emotionless except when it comes to rage. When it comes to sports, boys are expected to engage in contact sports such rugby, football and cricket; girls are typically expected to engage in non-contact sports such as netball and gymnastics.

Simon finds it difficult to speak definitively about where these expectations come from. It's a very existential question, he responds. Perhaps, he ponders, the expectations are as old as mankind, starting on the basis of human biology which makes men stereotypically physically stronger than women with men traditionally being providers because of their physical ability which means they historically went out to hunt or gather food, while women took on the stereotypical maternal roles. With more recent developments over time, he believes the segregation of responsibilities seem to be more of a social construct to suppress women and keep them in their place.

The Subordination & Suppression of Women

It does not make sense to Simon that women are suppressed. He reasons that women make up half of humans. We have the potential to make much more progress if we include everybody. He speculates that the suppression of women may be down to the fear of what would happen if women were provided with equal status to men. Perhaps there is a concern that women would eventually exceed men's status and this would be bad for men. He can't see any other possible reason for the thinking behind the suppression of women.

Simon acknowledges that while there are radical feminists who may see men as evil, there are other types of feminist, inclusive of liberal feminist who acknowledge there has been progress, but recognise that not enough has been done and are therefore pushing for further change. This makes sense to him; however, a lot of men seem to have been programmed to think that feminism represents the end of masculinity as we know it and the end of opportunities for men. He does not believe this is the case though; he is clear that it does not make sense for men and women to be as structurally divided as they currently are as one can't exist without the other. As a result one gender should not be disadvantaged while the other is advantaged.

Simon has gained a strong impression of the suppression/subordination of women from leadership in education where he has seen very few females in senior positions such as Headships and Heads of Departments. He's also observed a different atmosphere when females are teaching in classrooms from when male teachers are teaching.

Often, when male teachers walks into a classroom more respect it shown towards them than to female teachers when they walk into a class. He is pleased that in his house, his parents have an equal level of respect and feels lucky to experience equality at home, even though it's not reflected in wider society to the same degree.

The impression is that the impact of a patriarchal system and the subordination of women is carried through from a young age and school into adulthood and the workplace. Simon points to the saying, "You can't teach an old dog new tricks." He adds to this, that the tricks the dog has learnt come from continuous training. Just as a dog goes through continuous training to learn tricks, we learn from primary and secondary socialisation. For instance, he explains there is the primary socialisation from a home environment where boys are taught how to relate to the world. While he is fortunate to have been bought up in a positive environment, if a boy has a dad who is abusive to his mum, he may grow up not knowing better, thinking that's the way women should be treated and that it is manly to be abusive towards women. That may be all such men know. If they've grown up in such an environment, with such believes without being challenged, they are already invested in such habits. For a lot of men who have a lifelong habit of keeping women as subordinates, it may be difficult for them to see and accept the idea of equal rights. It's almost like saying Santa Claus doesn't exist. If Santa Claus doesn't exist and you don't put anything in his place, it doesn't feel equal to such a person and they are unlikely to want to engage in a conversation about equality as they don't see the alternative presented as beneficial to them in comparison to what they are used to. In their minds there may therefore be a question as to why they should invest in in an alternative which they believe changes the dynamics by creating more opportunities for females and less opportunities for men.

Simon believes it's beneficial to have both males and females in senior positions at work. Using the example of the education environment, he mentions that having female teachers is inspirational to girls. With males, it challenges what it means to be a female as it demonstrates that even though they may do things differently that females can do the same thing as males. He believes this will lead to a greater respect towards females, counteracting the patriarchy over time and leading to less thinking of women as subordinates. He believes that eliminating the gender divide will also help us to break down other divisions around other social constructs such as social class, race and religion. While he understands the human nature of wanting to have a community of like-minded people, he does not understand why we have to discriminate against people on the basis of difference.

The Limiting Factors
of a Patriarchal System

In a patriarchal system, males dominate and this can lead females to feel less than they are, with a sense that they can't achieve what they are actually capable of. The divisions caused in a patriarchal system also limit men. Men cannot do everything and so without women's input i.e. half of the human population, society and the human race as a whole is limited. The same would apply in a matriarchal society, explains Simon. A balance would be optimal, but what we have now is limiting and creates various social divisions that limit people's chances in life.

Simon further highlights, if for whatever reason a woman happens to be a single mother, because of the patriarch she would probably be earning less than her male counterparts. This may mean that her children are subjected to poverty though not as a reflection of the efforts of their mother who is likely to be working very hard. This would affect her male children just as much as female. As a result, an imbalanced system such as a patriarchy has the potential to limit everybody within the system.

Secondary Socialisation – The Church

Simon also speaks of the influence of secondary socialisation and influence that comes from external agencies such as school, religious organisation such as the Church and the public community. Focus in on religion and Abrahamic faiths – using Christianity as an example, he mentions he has noticed the masculine focus within the Bible such that not only are God and Jesus male, but most of the books in the Bible are written my men and those in positions of power were historically almost entirely male. This extended beyond the Church to the Royal Family where sons were supposed to carry the line. Although the Church no longer has as much influence on society as it used to when it was actually infused with politics, it is still part of society even if just in our subconscious and few people challenge it.

Intergenerational Society Norms

Simon believes a key reason why girls and boys are still expected and actively encouraged to behave in specified manners and follow defined paths in areas such as their choices of subjects is due to intergenerational society norms. This could be down to trivia such as a boy being told by his dad that he has to do maths, if not he's not a man.

There are efforts to bring about change in education with organisations such as "Girls into Science and Technology" and "Women

220

into Science and Engineering" that promote girls taking subjects and entering fields in STEM. From his point of view, while this has led to some progress, there is still an overwhelming majority of men entering such fields.

Simon additionally notes, there may be some members of staff and other children who have been raised with gendered expectations who encourage and influence other children with their expectations of how things should be. Children who do not naturally share their point of view may feel the need to meet these expectations in order to be accepted. As a result you have a whole community that still fosters the same old beliefs and practices.

Even though Simon recognises the progress that has been made, the patriarchal system that has come with the notion that women should be in domestic roles is centuries old. He therefore believes it may take up to 30-40 years to be able to see the real change arising from the measures currently being taken.

Challenging & Changing the System

Simon believes to bring about further changes to the system we need to influence children from an early age. He promotes the idea of doing subtle little things for children from birth to the age of four so they absorb and realise that both men and women are capable. He believes there is a need to challenge gender stereotypes right from nursery age as the older a person is the more difficult it is for change. He gives the example of the idea of having a girl as a superhero in some children's books: subtle changes that are stored in a child's sub-conscious that mean when they can consciously think of gender roles, they see males and females as less different. It would also make it a lot easier for children to accept and promote gender equality amongst their own circles and challenge gender stereotypes they may have been socialised to accept.

Simon also likes the idea of guests coming to school assemblies who are able to convey the message that men are great, but women are also great.. He would also like to see more examples of the positivity of women and how they have influenced the world to be shown in schools. As it stands, if you ask for the five best inventors, artists, actors etc people are likely to have been programmed to immediately think of men. He believes we will have made real progress when more people mention both males and females.

Celebrities & Successful People

From the visits of high profile women (and men) to his school and his wider observations, Simon believes they have the most positive impact when they command respect through their humility and a down to earth approach. This enables students to realise they are just like them and can achieve the same success. The most important thing with this is not just for the students to see the person, but to see through the interactions that they have been seen, leaving them with a greater sense of belief in themselves as it created a significant memory in people's mind which could have been the best thing that happened to them that day, week, month or even year. Ultimately creating the Obama style: "Yes You Can".

Against this backdrop, it's not surprise that the women that Simon find most inspiring are women who have determination and courage, and have the interesting and fortitude to support others.

A Fairer Society

Simon would like to see a fairer society with less division as he does not believe divisions help anyone. He believes that if it was ordained and natural for there to be a Gender Pay Gap, children would be able to recognise it. However, if you ask children – specially a boy if a girl should be paid the same for doing the same job, virtually all of them would say yes. He therefore questions what we think such inequalities will lead to in the future.

To Women: Old & Young

Simon has the genuine belief that women should not stop striving for greatness or stop pushing for equality or what is right.

If Simon had a sister, he'd tell her not to stop striving for greatness. He would probably feel the need to additionally tell her that things will be harder for her as she is female and black. He would, however, tell her not let what she can't control affect what she can control.

#Selah

Developing a Mosaic World

Recognising the Value of Women in the Workplace is a starting point. My ultimate objective is to develop a Mosaic World in which everyone's value is fully recognised in the workplace and beyond.

Do join me in the journey in Developing a Mosaic World.

Take the Mosaic survey to determine How Mosaic You Are.

The purchase of this book also provides you with two weeks free access to the Mosaic World Hub where you will find some valuable resources inclusive of some relevant links to information mentioned by some of the contributors.

www.MosaicWorld.live

References

1. Ajayi, O. A and Juma, M.K. (2009) *Gender Mainstreaming in Africa (2000-2008): Lessons Learnt and Opportunities for future Engage-ments, Femmes Africa Solidarite* (FAS), Geneva, New York and Dakar , 2009.
2. Ajayi, O.A. (2011) *Across the Spectrum of Development: Perspec-tives on Small Business, Trade, Reforms and Development,* Published by Top Range Nigeria Limited
3. Ajayi, O. A (2013) (Ed) *Reflection on Gender Equality in Africa; Status Report on the Implementation of Solemn Declaration on Gender Equality in Africa* Published by Femmes Africa Solidarite (FAS), Geneva, New York and Dakar
4. Ajayi, O.A (2016) *The Solemn Declaration Index (SDI)–Frame-work of the Performance Monitoring Index for the Implementation of SDGEA* Published by Gender Is My Agenda (GIMAC) Network with Support from United Nations Economic Commission for Africa (UNECA)
5. Ajayi, O. A. (2016) *From Adoption to Measurement- Measuring Gender Equality in Africa through the Application of Solemn Declaration Index and Scorecard,* 2016 Report of Gender Is My Agenda (GIMAC) Network
6. Ajayi, O. A. (2019) *Pushing the Frontier of Gender Equality in*

Africa, 2019 Report of Gender Is My Agenda (GIMAC) Network on the implementation of the Solemn Declaration on Gender Equality in Africa

7. Jack Zenger and Joseph Folkman Harvard research article: *Women Score Higher Than Men in Most Leadership Skills*

8. Chamorro-Premuzic, T (2019) *Why Do So Many Incompetent Men Become Leaders? (And How to Fix It)*

9. Nadwi, M.A. (2013) *al-Muhaddithat: the women scholars in Islam*. Interface Publications Ltd

About the Author

Susan is an award winning consultant specialising in Human Value in the workplace, education and wider society, a Community Activist with a deep-rooted belief in human value, a published author of books exploring the world in which we live in; and a Public Speaker.

Coming from a diverse, multicultural background with a diversity of experience from across different areas of society and involvement in different aspects of society, Susan has the ability to relate to and connect with people from a wide variety of backgrounds.

Susan Popoola runs Mosaic Fusions Ltd, a Business and Talent Development Support organisation which works with organisations to develop highly productive and fulfilling workplaces that reflect the rich diversity of society. She has extensive cross-sector experience inclusive of international experience working with organisations and delegates from Europe, Africa, the Middle East, China and the US.

Susan also runs Mosaic Wise, a Community Interest Company that works with individuals, education and organisations to support and enable Children and Young Adults to fully identify who they are and develop to be the best that they can be in the various environments and contexts they encounter in life.

The Value of Women at Work is Susan's third book. She has previously written *Touching the Heart of Milton Keynes: A Social Perspective*, *Consequences: Diverse to Mosaic Britain* and *The Value of Women at Work*.

Printed in Great Britain
by Amazon